ISRAEL'S
HOPE OF IMMORTALITY

FOUR LECTURES

BY THE

REV. C. F. BURNEY, M.A., D.Litt.

FELLOW AND LECTURER IN HEBREW OF ST. JOHN
BAPTIST'S COLLEGE, OXFORD

WIPF & STOCK · Eugene, Oregon

Wipf and Stock Publishers
199 W 8th Ave, Suite 3
Eugene, OR 97401

Israel's Hope of Immortality
Four Lectures
By Burney, C. F.
ISBN 13: 978-1-62564-938-6
Publication date 5/31/2014
Previously published by Oxford, 1909

PREFACE

THE four lectures contained in this volume were written for the Vacation Term for Biblical Study for Women, held at Durham in the summer of 1906, and are published by kind permission of the Editor of *The Interpreter*, in whose pages they appeared last year. The writer has made no attempt to enlarge the original scope and design of the lectures, which were necessarily limited; but he hopes that the book may prove useful as an illustration of the progressive character of the Old Testament Revelation, and may serve as an introduction to the study of larger works on the same subject.

C. F. B.

St. John's College,
Dec. 1908.

I

THE attempt to trace with some amount of exactitude the growth of a belief in a future life in the religion of Israel is an undertaking beset with no little difficulty.

We have to bear in mind that the materials at our disposal are far too scanty to allow of a clearly defined sketch of the lines of development; and we must beware of leaping to conclusions and then marshalling our evidence in proof by the aid of an imagination too facile at bridging the gaps which we must encounter. We must remember also—and this is a caution which has to be exercised in dealing with the growth of other religious beliefs both in Israel and among other races—that the evolution of the idea is, strictly speaking, logical rather than historical. I mean to say that the higher stages of thought are not invariably to be regarded as the later in time, as having developed out of and finally superseded the more crude. In the history of all intellectual processes it constantly happens that there arise minds which are above and in advance of the age which gives them birth; which overleap certain stages in the unfolding of truth, and rise at once to conceptions which may not become the common property of their race until perhaps generations have passed by and the intermediate stages of

thought have been slowly and ~~laboriously worked~~
out.   Thus we are likely to go astray if we attempt
to draw up a strictly chronological outline of the
development of this as of other religious beliefs.

One last caution remains. Those who believe
that in the Old Testament we have the record of
a revelation, partial and fragmentary indeed, but
divinely inspired and leading up to the mani-
festation of our Lord in the fullness of time, will
realize that in many cases the statements of
Old Testament writers and the ideas which they
embody are susceptible of a deeper significance
when read in the fuller light of New Testament
revelation.   Thus, for example, our Lord Himself
teaches that the words of revelation to Moses at
Horeb, ' I am the God of thy Father, the God of
Abraham, the God of Isaac, and the God of
Jacob,' contain implicitly the doctrine of a life
beyond the grave, since ' God is not the God
of the dead, but the God of the living '.   We are
not, however, at present concerned with this fuller
significance which may be read into the Old Testament Scriptures.   What we have to determine is
the character of certain conceptions at the time
at which they were enunciated, and the impression
which they produced upon those who heard and
debated, accepted or rejected them.

I do not, however, intend to imply by these
preliminary remarks that our sources are too
inadequate to enable us to determine the manner
in which belief in a future life came to form an

integral part of religious belief in Israel. There were in the history of the race great national crises which involved the breaking up of old ideas and the reconstruction of belief upon wider and sounder bases. A large part of Israel's literature groups itself about these periods of crisis and has to do with the vexed questions and phases of transition in religious thought which they involved. Thus we are able to trace broadly the progress of ideas from stage to stage, even where evidence is too slight and scanty to enable us to reconstruct in detail their historical evolution.

The Hope of a Future Life finds no Place in the Earlier Religion of Israel

Speaking generally, it may be said that the doctrine of immortality finds no place in the religious thought of Israel prior to the Exile. Certain ideas there were as to the state after death and the abode of the dead, but these belong to the common background of Semitic superstition, and have nothing to do with Israel's religion, the religion of Yahwe.

Among the Semites the abode of the departed was regarded as an underworld, i. e. it was located under the earth ; the conception of the earth being that of a more or less flat surface of land, surrounded by the sea and resting ultimately upon the watery abyss. The Hebrew title for this underworld is *She'ol*, a term of which the

etymology is unknown. Among the Babylonians
the name employed was the Sumerian KI-GAL,
the neo-Sumerian SHI-WAL, 'the great land,'
and it has been suggested with some plausibility
that She'ol may be a modified equivalent of this
Sumerian title.[1] In any case the Hebrew and
Babylonian conceptions of the character of the
place itself are essentially identical. The Hebrew
conception may aptly be illustrated from a passage in Job (x. 21–22) where the underworld is
described as

> A land of darkness and deep shade ;
> A land of gloom, like black darkness itself ;
> Deep shade without any order,
> And where the light is like black darkness.

The inhabitants of She'ol are spoken of as
Repha'im, a term which is best rendered 'shades',
meaning as it does 'relaxed' or 'flaccid' ones,
mere semblances of their former selves. The
existence of these beings in the underworld is
most vividly portrayed in a passage in the ' Taunt-
song ' against the King of Babylon in Isaiah xiv.
Here the fate of the king after death is brought
into salient contrast with his proud anticipation
of a future exaltation to the circle of the gods.

> She'ol from beneath is moved for thee to meet thee at
>   thy coming ;
> It stirreth up the shades for thee,
> Even all the chieftains of the earth,
> It hath raised up from their thrones all the kings of the
>   nations.

[1] For this suggestion the writer is indebted to Mr. C. J. Ball.

All of them shall answer and shall say unto thee,
Art *thou too* become weak like us, become like unto
   us ?
To She'ol is brought down thy pomp, the music of thy
   viols ;
Beneath thee is spread the maggot, and the worm
   covereth thee.
How art thou fallen from heaven, oh shining one, son of
   the morning,
How art thou cut down to the ground, that didst lay low
   the nations ?
And *thou*—thou saidst in thy heart, to heaven will I
   ascend,
Above the sfars of God will I exalt my throne ;
And I will sit upon the mount of assembly, in the utter-
   most parts of the north.
Yet unto She'ol shalt thou be brought down,
Unto the uttermost parts of the pit.
They that see thee shall narrowly look upon thee,
They shall consider thee closely ;
Is *this* the man who made the earth to tremble,
Who made kingdoms quake ?
Who made the world a wilderness, and overthrew its
   cities,
Who released not his prisoners to their home ?
All the kings of the nations, all of them,
Lie in honour, every one in his own house.
But thou art cast away from thy sepulchre like an
   abominable branch,
A garment of the slain that are thrust through with the
   sword,
That go down to the stones of the pit like a carcase
   trodden under foot.

   She'ol was pictured as ' the house of meeting
for all living ' (Job xxx. 23), good and bad without
distinction finding their abode there.

There the wicked cease from raging,
And the weary are at rest.
There the prisoners are at ease together,
They hear not the voice of the taskmaster.
The small and great are there ;
And the servant is free from his master.
—Job iii. 17–19.

The same conception of the underworld was current among the Babylonians. They pictured it as—

The gloomy house, the dwelling of the God Irkalla,
The house from which those who enter go not forth,
The road whose way is without return ;
The house whose enterers are deprived of light ;
Dust is their sustenance, their food is clay ;
Light they see not, in darkness they dwell ;
They are clad like birds with a garb of wings ;
Upon the door and its bolts there lies dust.
—*Keilinschriftliche Bibliothek* vi, p. 80.

We should gain no clear results were we to spend time in considering the relation conceived by the Hebrews as existing between body and soul or spirit. It is clear that She'ol is distinguished from the grave. The body rests in the grave, or is ignominiously cast forth ; the shade in any case is doomed to existence in She'ol. The shade, however, though disembodied, has a semblance of its former self by which it is recognizable. This we may gather from the extract which I have quoted which pictures the descent of the King of Babylon into She'ol. It is also clear from the narrative of Saul's visit to the witch of Endor, where the shade of Samuel, when raised, appears as 'an old man . . . covered with a garment' (I Sam. xxviii. 14). That some kind of relationship was conceived as existing between the dead body (buried or otherwise) and the shade in She'ol is probable. Burial in the family tomb, the being gathered to one's fathers, was desired as the final boon, and the carrying out of a father's wishes in this respect was the filial duty of his descendants. On the other hand, to be cast out unburied was the worst indignity which could be suffered : witness again' the Taunt-song against the King of Babylon, and Jeremiah's prophecy against Jehoiakim, King of Judah (Jer. xxii. 19). A remarkable passage in Job xiv. 21, 22 speaks of the dead man as though in She'ol he were dimly conscious of the gnawing pains of bodily corruption in the grave, though oblivious of all that goes on in the world from which he has been severed.

His sons come to honour, and he knoweth it not,
And they are brought low, but he perceiveth it not of them.
Only his flesh upon him hath pain,
And his soul upon him mourneth.

Intercourse between the living and the dead was sought among the Hebrews through the medium of necromancy. Thus the witch of Endor, who is described as 'mistress of a ghost'. or 'familiar spirit', is able by her art to raise the shade of Samuel, that he may be interviewed by Saul, and interrogated as to the future. The

term Yidh'ōni or ' knowing one ', as the repository
of such oracles, was applied sometimes to the
shade itself and sometimes to the medium who
was supposed to have the power of evokihg it.

Such necromancy was, however, forbidden by
Yahwe-religion. Deuteronomy xviii. 10, 11 for-
bids the existence in Israel of ' one that con-
sulteth a ghost or familiar spirit '; and it is
stated in 1 Samuel xxviii that Saul had put down
all such necromancers and that they were only
able to execute their art by stealth. In spite of
such prohibitions, it appears that necromancy was
largely practised during the period of the monarchy. Isaiah pictures it as the natural resource
of the Judeans in their national stress, as against
the word of Yahwe at the mouth of His prophet.

> And when they shall say unto you,
> Consult the ghosts and familiar spirits—
> On behalf of the living unto the dead,
> That chirp and that mutter !
> Should not a people consult their God,
> To get teaching and warning,
> And should they not believe in this word,
> Against which there is no counter-spell !
> —Isa. viii. 19, 20.[1]

That the practice of necromancy was connected with a cult of ancestor-worship which
flourished among the Hebrews the evidence is
practically *nil*.

[1] The passage as given above follows P. Ruben's rearrange-
ment of the text, with an emendation in line seven, יֹאמְרוּ בַּדָּבָר
in place of יֹאמְרוּ בַּדָּבָר.

Such being the views commonly held in Israel as to the state of existence after death, it may be understood that the outlook upon the unknown future was dreary and distasteful in the extreme. As I have already observed, this future state as thus conceived was entirely unconnected with the religion of Yahwe. It was this that caused the keenest poignancy of despair to pious souls to whom in the present their relationship to Yahwe meant much. Thus in Hezekiah's poem, after his recovery from mortal sickness, we find the words :—

For She'ol cannot praise Thee, death cannot celebrate Thee.
They that go down into the pit cannot hope for Thy faithfulness.
The living, the living, he shall praise Thee as I do this day.
—Isa. xxxviii. 18, 19.

Or again, we find a Psalmist exclaiming :—

For in death there is no remembrance of Thee,
In She'ol who shall give Thee thanks ?—Ps. vi. 5.

The dead praise not Yahwe,

says another poet,

Neither all they that go down into silence.—Ps. cxv. 17.

While yet another, in his despondency, describes himself as

Cast off among the dead,
Like the slain that lie in the grave,
Whom Thou rememberest no more ;
And they are cut off from Thy hand.—Ps. lxxxviii. 5.

And the same writer exclaims :—

Wilt Thou do wonders for the dead ?
Or shall the shades arise and give Thee thanks ?
Shall Thy kindness be told in the grave ?
Thy faithfulness in the place of destruction ?
Shall Thy wonders be known in the dark ?
And Thy righteousness in the land of forgetfulness ?

Passages such as these remind us forcibly of the Greek conception of the joyless condition of existence after death, as voiced by the shade of Achilles :—

βουλοίμην κ' ἐπάρουρος ἐὼν θητευέμεν ἄλλῳ,
ἀνδρὶ παρ' ἀκλήρῳ, ᾧ μὴ βίοτος πολὺς εἴη,
ἢ πᾶσιν νεκύεσσι καταφθιμένοισιν ἀνάσσειν.
                                        —*Od.* xi. 489–491.

Rather I'd choose laboriously to bear
A weight of woes, and breathe the vital air,
A slave to some poor hind that toils for bread,
Than reign the sceptred monarch of the dead.

The Reason why Early Yahwe-religion Lacked a Doctrine of a Future Life

If we now inquire the reason of the failure of early Yahwe-religion to extend beyond the present life and to illuminate the gloom of the future state, we shall find it no doubt in the fact that, prior to the eighth century B. C. (i. e. the century which witnessed the labours of the first writing prophets, Amos and Hosea, Isaiah and Micah), the old-time conception of Yahwe was strictly national. Yahwe-worship, at this stage, is best described as *monolatry* rather than *monotheism*. Yahwe was Israel's only God, and the obligation to worship Him and Him only was clear to His faithful adherents ; but this did not hinder the belief that other nations might in like manner have *their own* national deities who had as real an existence as had Yahwe, though Israel was bound to these extraneous deities by no tie, and owed them no sort of allegiance.[1] The conception of the state for Israel as for their neighbours was *theocratic*, i. e. the national God was regarded as *King* of His people, the earthly king as vicegerent of the national God. When war was carried on it was waged against the God of the hostile nation, quite as much as against the nation itself and its human monarch, and the national God was leader of His forces to battle against the Deity of the opposing army. Thus we find that Israel's national Deity Yahwe is particularly associated with the battlefield. He is Yahwe Sèbha'oth, the God of armies, to whom is due success in battle. It is in accordance with this conception that we find that the call to arms was constantly the occasion for the revival of the national spirit of allegiance to Yahwe, after periods of religious decadence. Further, the fact is closely bound up with this conception of Yahwe as national Deity that the nation and not the individual was regarded as the religious unit. The relation between Yahwe and Israel was pictured under the form of a

[1] Cf. the writer's *Outlines of Old Testament Theology*, pp. 34 ff.

covenant, and to this covenant the parties were Yahwe on the one side and the nation on the other. The idea that covenant relationship existed between the Deity and individual Israelites as such seems to have been foreign to the religious conception so long as the view maintained that Yahwe was strictly the national Deity only. It is true that, at its foundation, Yahwe's covenant was pictured as concluded with individuals, in the persons of Israel's ancestors, Abraham, Isaac and Jacob. But these figures were idealized as the founders of the nation, and represented to later thought the religious unity of the nation as a party to the covenant. Indeed, the fact that the covenant was believed to have been once for all concluded by Yahwe with Israel's righteous ancestors tended to emphasize the conception that it was a national covenant and to minimize the rights of the individual. Framed once for all with Abraham as the religious unit upon the human side, the covenant was independent of infringement upon the part of individual members of the nation in later times. Such infringement involved the cutting off of the sinner from the nation and from the rights of the covenant, but it could not in any way abrogate the covenant itself. However great and widespread might be the growth of apostasy and the failure to live up to the covenant terms at any particular age, yet it never could become universal. There always must be found the righteous nucleus within the nation which held fast to the terms of relationship with Yahwe, the 'seven thousand in Israel, every knee which has not bowed unto Baal and every mouth which has not kissed him'; and this righteous nucleus was the true Israel, the true nation with whom the covenant stood fast. Had this not been the case, i. e. had apostasy ever become universal so as to have embraced the whole nation and to have involved the abrogation of the national covenant, then Yahwe would have proved Himself unfaithful to the covenant made once for all with faithful Abraham, a contingency in itself impossible and utterly to be repudiated as such by the national conscience.

The same point of view governed the conception of the Divine covenant with David. Made once for all with David as 'the man after God's own heart', it involved the promise that David was always to have 'a lamp' before Yahwe, the quenchless flame being emblematic of a perpetual posterity to sit upon his throne.[1] This covenant, however, did not hinder the possibility that individual members of David's line might fail in their responsibilities and pay the penalty which unfaithfulness involved. Only they could not, through their sins, abrogate the covenant with David's line. This again was impossible under the terms of the covenant. The covenant was with David as representative of the dynasty; it

---

[1] Cf., for the emblematic use of the expression in this connexion, 1 Kings xi. 36, xv. 4, 2 Kings viii. 19, Ps. cxxxii. 17.

was not with any individual member of the dynasty as an individual. This conception of the Davidic covenant is well illustrated by the words of Psalm lxxxix. 28–37 :—

> My mercy will I keep for him for evermore,
> And My covenant shall stand fast with him.
> His seed also will I make to endure for ever,
> And his throne as the days of heaven.
> If his children forsake My law,
> And walk not in My judgements ;
> If they break My statutes,
> And keep not My commandments ;
> Then will I visit their transgression with the rod,
> And their iniquity with stripes.
> But My mercy will I not utterly take from him,
> Nor suffer My faithfulness to fail.
> My covenant will I not break,
> Nor alter the thing that is gone out of My lips.
> Once have I sworn by My holiness ;
> I will not lie unto David ;
> His seed shall endure for ever,
> And his throne as the sun before Me.
> It shall be established for ever as the moon,
> And as the faithful witness in the sky.

THE NATION THE RELIGIOUS UNIT

I have dealt at some length with this conception of the nation as the religious unit because it seems to me that it requires thinking over in order to be apprehended, and that when apprehended it explains much in connexion with our subject which might otherwise remain obscure. The nation as such did not die, and therefore there was no question of the Divine covenant being annulled by death. The individual as such had no rights within the covenant : he was only a member of his clan which was a portion of the nation, and so he shared indirectly in the blessings of the national covenant so long as he continued to live up to its enactments. But the idea of individualism was always at this stage merged in collectivism. There was nothing repugnant to the religious conscience of the time that Yahwe should ' visit the sins of the fathers upon the children unto the third and fourth generation '. Achan might by his trespass involve the destruction of his whole family, and Divine justice, so far from being impugned by the event, was in fact regarded as vindicated by it.

We gather then that the religious ideal of early times, great and lofty as it was in its assertion of the indestructibility of the Divine covenant with Israel, and capable of almost indefinite develop- ment in the hands of the later prophets, was at this stage very partial and one-sided, and, con- centrating itself upon the nation, it had little to offer to the individual. If in this life he had no standing in relationship with Yahwe in virtue of his distinct personality, what could he expect to possess in the state after death, to which, according to the conception of his time, Yahwe's activities were not extended ?

Rudiments of a Doctrine of Immortality in Early Times

It would, however, probably be a mistake to imagine that because, at the stage with which we are dealing, Israel's religion had nothing to offer to the individual in the way of a hope of a future life beyond the grave, therefore there was a complete acquiescence in this blank prospect, and men's minds never rose in aspiration to anything higher. There are a few passages in writings of a comparatively early date which may be said to contain the rudiments of a doctrine of immortality in so far as they picture the possibility of immortality as presenting itself, to the mind of the writers. Such is the reference in Genesis iii. 22 (the narrative of the Fall by the prophetical writer J) to the tree of life which grew in Eden, whereof if man's first parents had eaten they might have lived for ever. Just the same conception occurs in the Babylonian Epic of Gilgameš. Gilgameš, in search of immortality, wins his way with great difficulty to the abode of Nuḫ-napištim, a man who, once human, has been raised by the gods to a place among the immortals, and who therefore may be hoped to possess the secret of immortality, if he can be prevailed upon to transmit it. Nuḫ-napištim relates to Gilgameš his strange story, which is the Babylonian counterpart of the Hebrew flood narrative (Nuḫ-napištim corresponding to Noaḥ), and finally explains how that, after his escape from the flood in the ship which he had built, he was raised to immortality by the gods together with his wife, and made to dwell ' in the distance, at the confluence of the streams ', a locality which seems to correspond in its main conceptions to the Biblical Eden. The best that Nuḥ-napištim can do for Gilgameš is to direct him to search for a magic herb, called *šibu issaḥir amêlu*, i. e. ' (When) old a man becomes young '. Those who eat of this herb will attain immortality. Gilgameš is fortunate enough to discover and pluck the herb, but shortly afterwards, whilst he is bathing, a serpent snatches it away, and he loses for ever the chance of immortality which has actually come within his grasp. Both this story and the Hebrew story, which probably have their roots far back in a common source, illustrate the fact that there existed early speculations as to man's failure to obtain the immortality which was the lot of the gods.

We may notice also, in the earlier literature of Israel, the legends of the translations of Enoch and Elijah, individual cases in which men were believed to have escaped death and to have been raised to the society of God. There was not, however (so far as we have evidence) any argument from the particular to the general. Enoch, like Nuḥ-napištim, was a mysterious personage who on account of his piety had been raised above the common lot of humanity. Among the

Babylonians certain of the early kings appear with the determinative of deity prefixed to their names ; and the expectation of exaltation to the mountain of the gods is pictured as filling the mind of the King of Babylon in the ' Taunt-song ' of Isaiah xiv which I have already quoted :—

> And *thou*—thou saidst in thy heart,
> 　To heaven will I ascend,
> Above the stars of God will I exalt my throne ;
> And I will sit upon the mount of assembly,
> In the uttermost parts of the north.

Such speculations as these, however, were, as may well be understood, far removed from any hope of a brighter future as the lot of ordinary humanity.

FACTORS IN THE DEVELOPMENT OF A DOCTRINE OF A FUTURE LIFE

We now have to notice the main factors which brought about a break-up in old conceptions and a further and higher development of religious thought in regard to the subject with which we are dealing.

I. *The Rise of the Doctrine of Monotheism*

The most important of these was the rise and development of the doctrine of *monotheism* in the eighth century B. C. Yahwe, hitherto the national God of Israel, becomes henceforth the God of the whole earth. The national gods of the nations around come to be no gods, mere idols, the work of men's hands.

When we associate the doctrine of Yahwe as the only God of the whole earth with the activity of the writing prophets of the middle and later part of the eighth century B. C., it does not follow that such a conception was hitherto altogether unthought of by higher minds in Israel. The prophetical narrative of the Creation (Gen. ii. 4 ff., part of the document which we distinguish by the symbol J) pictures Yahwe-Elohim as the Creator of the world ; and the date of this narrative, even in its present form, is doubtless to be carried back considerably earlier than the middle of the eighth century. Still, such a conception does not appear at an earlier stage to have been pressed home to its logical conclusion and to have influenced religious thought in general. When Amos propounded his doctrine that Yahwe had relations with the surrounding nations, and would judge them and Israel alike in accordance with their observance of a common standard of morality, his teaching must have fallen as an entirely new conception upon the minds of those to whom it was presented. *They* thought that because Yahwe was their national God He must be ready in the long run to favour and maintain His people in spite of moral laxity and a mere formal standard of religion ; but the prophet argued that special privilege involved special responsibility, and that failure to discharge this debt would involve

punishment even so severe as the destruction of
the offenders : ' You only have I known of all
the families of the earth : therefore will I visit
upon you all your iniquities ' (Amos iii. 2).

The doctrine that Yahwe was no mere national
God, but the only God, as developed by Amos,
carried with it the truth that He was the maker
and sustainer of the world, and the one supreme
arbiter of men's thoughts and deeds.   No part of
the universe was beyond the reach of His hand,
and so none could escape His power. 'Though
they dig into She'ol, thence shall My hand take
them ; and though they climb up into heaven,
thence will I bring them down.   And though they
hide themselves in the top of Carmel, I will search
and take them out thence ; and though they be
hid from My sight in the bottom of the sea, thence
will I command the serpent, and he shall bite
them ' (Amos ix. 3).

Isaiah, a few years later than Amos, carries on
the same monotheistic teaching in the southern
kingdom.   The majesty and holiness of Yahwe
forms the theme upon which he works, and his
favourite title for Yahwe is ' The Holy One of
Israel '.   Speaking of the day of Yahwe Seba'oth,
i. e. the day of His vengeance upon all that is
repugnant to His holiness, he tells his hearers that
' Yahwe alone shall be exalted in that day.   And
the idols shall utterly pass away ' (Isa. ii. 17, 18).
The Assyrian, though he knows it not, is merely
a rod in Yahwe's hand for the execution of His

vengeance upon the nations, and he in turn must
suffer punishment for the haughty insolence with
which he magnifies himself against Yahwe (Isa.
x. 5 ff.).

If we seek along the historical horizon of the
time for a reason why the monotheistic idea should
have claimed prominence at just this stage in
Israel's national life, our gaze must be arrested
by the rapid progress of the Assyrian conquests.
The spectacle of nations and their gods one after
another falling helpless before the conqueror's
resistless power may well have influenced the
moulding of prophetic thought both in Israel and
Judah. On the other hand, the reason why
Isaiah should have anticipated any other fate for
the small kingdom of Judah than that which
had befallen the surrounding nations can be
explained as nothing else than the Divine intuition
which belonged to him as Yahwe's prophet. And
the brilliant fulfilment of his predictions in the
sudden arrest of the Assyrian's progress before
the gates of Jerusalem must have gone far to
confirm in the popular mind the truth of his
assertion that Yahwe, and He alone, is the God
of the whole earth, who holds the fate of nations
in His hand.

We may then regard the establishment of the
doctrine of monotheism as the first great advance
in the direction of a higher conception as to the
future state. If Yahwe is supreme Deity of the
Universe, then She'ol also must be found to come

within the range of His hand, and its inhabitants need not be regarded as outside His care. These are inferences which now first emerge as possibilities; though, as we shall see, they do not appear to have been worked out to their conclusion until a long subsequent age.

II. *The Rise of the Doctrine of Religious Individualism*

The second important factor towards an advance in thought was the decline and downfall of the Judean kingdom in the early part of the sixth century B. C. The decay and destruction of the *nation* brought into prominence Yahwe's relation to the *individual*. At this period the great religious teacher was the prophet Jeremiah, and he may be regarded as the founder of the doctrine of religious individualism. Jeremiah laboured under no misapprehension as to the fate of the Judean kingdom. He clearly foresaw that its downfall and destruction were inevitable, and all his counsels made for unconditional submission to the Chaldean, a line of advice which brought down upon him the charge of disaffection, and rendered him so unpopular in Jerusalem that his life was more than once in grave danger.

Like the prophets who preceded him, Jeremiah looked forward to the establishment in the future of an ideal Messianic kingdom, after the chastisement so nearly impending had done its work, and the iniquity of his people had been purged away. But the moral regeneration of the people must come about through the realization of the moral responsibility of the individual. The old idea, under which, as we have seen, the nation, not the individual, was the unit, had been tersely expressed in the popular proverb, ' The fathers have eaten sour grapes, and the children's teeth are set on edge ' (Jer. xxxi. 29). This proverb summed up the view of Divine justice which conceived the sins of the father to be visited on the children unto the third and fourth generation, a view which, with our knowledge of heredity and other social factors, we see to have a one-sided approximation to truth, but the glaring injustice of which as an inexorable law must tend to come into prominence so soon as the responsibility and rights of the individual begin to be realized. And the employment of the proverb itself suggests that the sense of this injustice had begun to assert itself in the popular mind. In the future, says Jeremiah, this proverb shall no more be used : ' But every one shall die for his own iniquity : every man that eateth sour grapes, his teeth shall be set on edge.'

And then follows the magnificent conception of the new covenant, unlike the former covenant with the nation at large which was graven on tables of stone, but written upon the hearts of its individual recipients : ' This is the covenant which I will make with the house of Israel after those days, saith Yahwe ; I will put My law in their inward parts, and in their heart will I write it ; and I will be their God, and they shall be My people : and they shall teach no more every man his neighbour, and every man his brother, saying, Know Yahwe : for they shall all know Me, from the least of them unto the greatest of them, saith Yahwe ; for I will forgive their iniquity, and their sin will I remember no more ' (Jer. xxxi. 33, 34).

The truth of individual responsibility, thus enunciated, was not allowed to fall to the ground. Ezekiel was one of the captives who had been carried into Babylonia with Jehoiachin in B. C. 597. He received his prophetic call in the fifth year of the captivity of Jehoiachin (B. C. 592), and the latest date in his book falls twenty-two years later (B. C. 570). He thus appears as a somewhat younger contemporary of Jeremiah ; and he was carrying on his prophetic work among the exiles already in Babylonia whilst Jeremiah was endeavouring to gain a hearing in the doomed city of Jerusalem. Ezekiel (ch. xviii) takes up the same proverb of the sour grapes, and, like Jeremiah, he asserts that Israel shall in the future have no occasion to use it, supporting his contention by a series of elaborately worked out instances illustrative of the truth of the responsibility of the individual.

We may take it then, that it was at the crisis of the downfall of the Judean kingdom that the old idea of the nation as the religious unit began to be superseded by the view that the individual stood in a position of moral relationship towards Yahwe and was to be judged in accordance with his own deserts. With this step in advance there were opened up new possibilities of development in the doctrine of man's relationship to God, not merely in the present life but in the unseen state beyond the grave.

II

In the previous lecture we reached a point at which the conception of the responsibilities and rights of the individual first appear to have become clearly established. Yahwe's word, by the mouth of Ezekiel, is ' Behold, all souls are mine : as the soul of the father, so also the soul of the son is mine : the soul that sinneth, it shall die ' (xviii. 4). And the conclusion emphasizes Jeremiah's conception of the new covenant, written upon the hearts of its individual recipients : ' Therefore I will judge you, O house of Israel, every one according to his ways, saith Yahwe-Elohim. Return ye, and turn yourselves from all your transgressions ; so iniquity shall not be your ruin. Cast away from you all your transgressions, wherein ye have transgressed ; and make you a new heart and a new spirit ; for why will ye die, O house of Israel ? For I have no pleasure in the death of him that dieth, saith Yahwe-Elohim : Wherefore turn yourselves and live ' (Ezek. xviii. 30–32).

Religious individualism, then, at this stage, involves that the individual stands in such a moral relationship to Yahwe that righteousness on his part must meet with its due reward, and iniquity with its due punishment. Still, however, the view of man's relationship to his God appears sharply limited by the span of this present life. There is

as yet no conception of its continuity into the
unknown future. Thus, in order that Yahwe's
moral dealing with man may justify itself under
this conception, it follows that in this life righteousness must be observed to meet with reward,
and wickedness with punishment. This is a
theory which, like others which we have noticed,
has a rough and general approximation to truth.
Society being constituted as it is, it usually happens
under normal conditions that moral and social
rectitude meets with its recompense in this life.
A life framed in accordance with God's moral laws
is likely on the whole to be immune from the ills
which attack the dissolute, and to be prolonged
to old age, and commercial integrity and fair dealing between man and man most often in the long
run command success. On the other hand, it
happens normally that the sinner pays the penalty
of his wickedness, it may be by disease and death
brought on by a vicious career, by business-failure,
or by punishment at the hands of the law.

It was impossible, however, that such a theory
should for long escape challenge. Glaring exceptions to the established rule were always likely to
occur. More especially would this be the case at
such a period as the fall of the Judean Monarchy,
the Exile in Babylon, and the Restoration, when
upright and pious men formed a minority, often
despised and sometimes persecuted, when patriotic
hopes kindled by the return from captivity were
destined speedily to disappointment, and to the

witness of ' the day of small things ' as against
the expectations of a glorious future which had
been kindled by the prophets. We find then that
the problem of the undeserved suffering of the
righteous and the unchecked prosperity of the
wicked excited a large amount of speculation and
religious difficulty at the period which we have
now reached ; and it was out of this soil that the
idea of personal immortality appears to have
arisen, at times as an aspiration or merely tenta-
tive solution of the anomalies of the present life,
at times as a dearly prized conviction of individual
hearts, but not yet as a definitely formulated
dogma of religion.

THE PROBLEM OF SUFFERING IN RELATION TO THE HOPE OF IMMORTALITY

We must now, therefore, proceed to consider
the Hebrew literature which concerns itself with
this subject, and endeavour to ascertain as precisely as we can what was in the mind of the
writers, and how far they were able to unravel to
their own satisfaction the difficulties which presented themselves to their thought.

It is remarkable that Jeremiah, who, as we have
noticed, was the first to formulate the conception
of the relationship of the individual to Yahwe and
his judgement in accordance with his deserts, is
also the first to be perplexed and troubled by the

apparent breakdown of this theory as worked out in his experience. It is remarkable, I say, and yet scarcely to be wondered at; for Jeremiah is the most intensely human of all Old Testament writers. We find contending in him the alternations of confidence and despair: at one time he is filled with perfect joy in communion with God, at another with utter despondency and the very blackness of loneliness and desolation; at one time he is transformed by enthusiasm for his mission, at another cast down to the depths by its apparent futility, and pierced to the quick by the gibes and insults which it is his lot to bear. Thus the failure of his theory of religion, the apparent prosperity of the wicked in spite of his sin, presents itself to him as a painful anomaly. 'Righteous art Thou, Yahwe,' he exclaims, 'when I plead with Thee: yet would I reason the cause with Thee: wherefore doth the way of the wicked prosper? Wherefore are all they at ease that deal very treacherously? Thou hast planted them, yea, they have taken root; they grow, yea, they bring forth fruit: Thou art near in their mouth, and far from their reins.' All that he can hope is that Yahwe will in the long run vindicate His righteousness. He continues, 'But Thou, Yahwe, knowest me; Thou seest me and triest mine heart toward Thee: pull them out like sheep for the slaughter, and prepare them for the day of slaughter' (Jer. xii. 1–3).

The Psalms

But it is in the Psalms that the problem of suffering Righteousness repeatedly presents itself, in the mouths of poets speaking either for themselves as individuals, or as representatives of a class—the meek, or afflicted ones. In the large majority of cases no attempt is made at a solution of undeserved suffering ; the psalm takes the form of a prayer addressed to Yahwe, not a treatise for the edification of suffering Israel. The conviction is often expressed that Yahwe will vindicate the cause of His servants in this life sooner or later, and will punish the cruelty and arrogance of the wicked.

If I had not trusted to behold the goodness of Yahwe in the land of the living !—

exclaims one Psalmist (xxvii. 13) breaking off in an aposiopesis, which our English Version with a correct approximation to the sense of the suppressed apodosis, though with some weakening of the force of the original, supplies by insertion of the words ' I should utterly have fainted '.

For Thou hast delivered my soul from death,

says another,

That I may walk before God in the light of the living
—lvi. 13.

As for the wicked, the conviction is expressed that—

Thou, Yahwe, shalt bring them down to the hole of the pit ;
The men of bloodshed and guile shall not live out half their days—(Ps. lv. 23).

Two Psalms, xvi and xvii, end by expression of the writers' trust in Yahwe in terms which have been thought to express conviction of a blessed future beyond the grave. Let us examine them. Psalm xvi finishes with the words :—

I have set Yahwe before me continually,
Because He is at my right hand, I shall not be moved,
Therefore my heart is glad, and my glory rejoiceth ;
My flesh also dwelleth in security.
For Thou will not abandon my soul to She'ol,
Thou wilt not suffer Thy godly one to see the pit.
Thou makest me to know the path of life,
Fulness of joys is in Thy presence,
In Thy right hand there are pleasures for evermore.

Now though the Prayer-book Version of these words suggests almost irresistibly a reference to the life beyond the grave, and though it is most fit that the words should be used by Christians in the fuller sense which further Revelation has secured for them, yet it must be concluded, on examination of the terms employed by the Psalmist, that it was not in his mind to formulate any definite belief as to a future life. The rendering of verse 9[b] in Prayer-book Version and Authorized Version, ' My flesh also shall rest in hope,' can scarcely fail to suggest a reference to the body lying in the grave in expectation of a future resurrection. Such an explanation is, however, impossible. The term in Hebrew which is rendered ' My flesh ', בְּשָׂרִי is only employed of the *living* body ; and the Psalmist is simply stating that, in his confidence in Yahwe's protection, he can live his life without fear of dangers which may assail him. Again, verse 10 must not be rendered, ' Thou wilt not leave my soul in She'ol,' but, as I have already given it, ' Thou wilt not abandon my soul to She'ol,' i.e. Yahwe will rescue his life from the imminent danger of physical death to which it is exposed. We may compare Psalm xxx. 3, where the same idea is expressed :—

Yahwe, Thou hast brought up my soul from She'ol,
Thou hast kept me alive, that I should not go down to
     the pit.

I believe, however, that this Psalm, if it does not formulate any doctrine of immortality, at least strikes the key-note upon which the belief is based. ' The path of life ' which Yahwe makes known to His servant means life with God as distinct from mere earthly existence which man shares in common with the brute-creation. In face of all that this means to him, and in the bliss of the felt communion with his God, the poet seems, for the moment at least, to overlook the fact of death, and he is able to speak of the pleasures in Yahwe's right hand as enduring ' for evermore '.

The passage in Psalm xvii which comes under consideration is the last verse :—

But as for me, in righteousness may I behold Thy face !
May I be satisfied, when I awake, with Thy likeness !

Here the interpretation turns on the sense which is attached to the expression 'When I awake'. It is natural for us, as Christians, to see in it an

allusion to the awakening from death conceived
as a sleep. But that such an idea was in the
mind of the Psalmist is more than doubtful.
More probably he is simply expressing the desire
that morning by morning, as he awakes to the
daily round, he may do so with a renewed sense
of Yahwe's fatherly care. This is the sense which
is supported by consideration of parallel passages.
So we have Psalm iii. 5 :—

> I laid me down and slept ;
> *I awaked* ; for Yahwe sustaineth me.

And again, another poet says :—

How precious are Thy thoughts unto me, O God !
How great is the sum of them !
If I should count them, they are more in number than
    the sand :
When I awake, I am still with Thee.—Ps. cxxxix. 17, 18.

In the same way, Proverbs vi. 22, in speaking
of the value of a parent's teaching, remarks :—

> When thou walkest, it shall lead thee ;
> When thou liest down, it shall watch over thee ;
> And *when thou awakest*, it shall talk with thee.

We may conclude, therefore, that it is too
precarious to read any hope of immortality into
the words ' When I awake ' in Psalm xvii. 17.

There are certain Psalms which definitely set
themselves to unravel the problem of the suffering
of the righteous and the prosperity of the wicked.
These we must examine.

In Psalm xxxvii the poet takes his stand upon

the contention that the moral anomaly presented by the problem is merely temporary. In the long run wickedness will be punished and righteousness rewarded. The opening stanzas of the Psalm strike the key-note of the theme which is developed throughout :—

Fret not thyself because of the ungodly,
Neither be thou envious of the workers of iniquity ;
For they shall soon be mown down like the grass,
And like the green herbage shall they fade.
'Trust in Yahwe, and do good,
Dwell in the land and follow after faithfulness ;
So shalt thou delight thyself in Yahwe,
And He shall grant thee the petitions of thy heart.
Commit thy way unto Yahwe ;
And trust in Him, and He shall act.
And He shall bring forth as the light thy righteous-
    ness,
And thy just right as the noonday.

In fact, the writer is so thoroughly convinced that the problem meets with its adequate solution in this life that he makes no exceptions to the rule of retributive justice. His experience, briefly stated, is :—

I have been young and now am old,
Yet saw I never the righteous forsaken nor his seed
    begging bread.

On the other hand :—

I have seen the wicked like a terrible one,
And putting forth his strength like a spreading
    cedar.
But I passed by and lo, he was not ;
When I sought him, he could not be found.

The conclusion is :—

> Mark the perfect man, and behold the upright,
> For there is a posterity to the man of peace.
> But transgressors shall be destroyed together ;
> The posterity of the wicked shall be cut off.

As we read the Psalm, we cannot help feeling that, when we have paid full tribute to the writer's strong religious faith, yet he must have been a man of extraordinary optimism or have been placed in such a situation that he did not fully realize the anomalies of the present. In any case, the iron does not seem to have entered into his soul as it did into the souls of certain other Psalmists ; consequently we look in vain for any hint that the unseen future beyond the grave may offer a solution which this earthly stage taken by itself is unable to afford.

We pass on to Psalm xlix, where the writer develops the same theme. His language and outlook are modelled upon that of the so-called ' Wisdom ' literature of Israel, and present many parallels to the Books of Proverbs and Job. At the outset he abandons the national standpoint, and proclaims himself a citizen of the world. His message is a philosophy of life which has universal application, and so he addresses it to humanity at large :—

> O hear ye this, all ye peoples ;
> Give ear, all ye that dwell in the fleeting age ;
> Both sons of mean man and sons of high man ;
> Rich and poor together.

He then propounds his ' problem ' or ' enigma '—
the prosperity of the worldly wicked :—

They that trust in their wealth,
And boast themselves of the multitude of their riches.

The point which he emphasizes is that all this
earthly prosperity is sharply terminated by death,
and that at this crisis it can avail a man nothing
for the ransom of his life.   However wide his acres
may be, and however arrogantly he may give his
name to his estate, under the fond impression that
it will belong to his posterity for ever, yet he
himself can look forward to an estate no wider
than the grave, and to the cheerless prospect of
She'ol :—

But surely [1] no man can ransom himself,
Or give to God the price of his life—
For the ransom of their life is too costly,
And one must let that alone for ever—
That he should live on for ever,
And not see the pit.
For he seeth that wise men die,
Together the self-confident and brutish perish,
And leave their wealth for others.
Their graves [2] are their houses for ever,
Their habitations to all generations,
Even of them that called estates after their own names.
For man in honour hath no abiding ;
He is like the beasts which perish.

In continuance, the lot of the wicked is contrasted

---

[1] Reading אַךְ לֹא פָרֹה יִפְדֶּה אִישׁ in place of the Hebrew text
which is rendered in R.V., 'None of them can by any means
redeem his brother.'

[2] קָבְרָם or קְבָרִים in place of קִרְבָּם.

with that of the righteous, in language which is
somewhat obscure in detail, but of which the
general drift seems to be clear :—

This is the fate of them that have self-confidence,
And of those who following them approve their speech.
Like a flock they are placed (ready) for She'ol ;
Death is their shepherd ;
And the upright have dominion over them in the morning ;
And their form must She'ol consume, that there be no
    habitation for it.
But surely God will ransom my life from the hand of
    She'ol ;
For He will take me.

Here again the question arises whether the
Psalmist is expressing his conviction of a blessed
immortality for the righteous, or whether the final
triumph of the righteous is conceived as taking
place in this life and so tacitly limited to it.   The
majority of scholars take this latter view ; but
personally, the more I examine this Psalm the
more does the conviction force itself upon me
that the writer has in view something more than
the mere temporary recompense of the righteous
during this earthly life.   The interpretation turns
largely upon the meaning which is given to the
expression 'In the morning', as describing the
time at which the righteous are ' to have dominion '
over the wicked, i.e. to witness the vindication of
their righteousness.   The expression is thought by
many to have merely temporal reference to the
dawning of happier times for the upright after the
destruction of the wicked as described in Malachi

iv. 1–3 : 'Behold, the day cometh, it burneth as a furnace, and all the proud, and all that work wickedness shall be stubble : and the day that cometh shall burn them up, saith Yahwe of hosts, that it shall leave them neither root nor branch. But unto you that fear My name shall the sun of righteousness arise with healing on His wings ; and ye shall go forth and gambol as calves of the stall. And ye shall tread down the wicked ; for they shall be ashes under the soles of your feet in the day that I do make, saith Yahwe of hosts.'

Against this view, it seems to me that nowhere in the Psalm does the writer predict any sudden and overwhelming calamity as impending upon the wicked. Throughout, the point which he emphasizes is that, however prosperous his life may be, yet death is bound to end all. Death is conceived as the inevitable which cannot be bought off with worldly riches ; but the idea of death falling as a sudden and unexpected blow upon the ungodly is foreign to the whole conception ; since the writer sets himself to propound facts of human experience which must be obvious to all who will think about them, and the view that the worldly wicked are specially doomed to a sudden visitation of death in the form of a dire calamity is not one of these. The view of death as the inevitable issue of life, uninfluenced by riches and worldly position, is rounded off by the refrain of verse 12 :—

For man in honour hath no abiding ;
He is like the beasts which perish ;

and it is in the next section that the Psalmist passes beyond experience, and expresses the conviction of faith as to the future in store for the righteous. If, then, the wicked are to meet their retribution by no sudden blow, but simply by death as the end of all their pomp and circumstance, then it seems that the prediction of something different in store for the righteous *must* contain more than the expectation of their vindication in this life only. The striking definiteness of the expression ' In the morning ' almost inevitably suggests to us a reference to the Resurrection morning ; though, in our ignorance of the date of the Psalm and the background of belief which the writer had behind him, we can affirm nothing definite with regard to it. In verse 15 the statement—

God shall ransom my soul from the hand of She'ol,
For He *shall take me*,

recalls to mind the account of Enoch's translation: ' He was not, *for God took him*,' the same Hebrew verb being used in each case. If, as seems very probable, the Psalmist is choosing his words with reference to this narrative, then the conclusion follows almost necessarily that he is looking forward to a deliverance from She'ol which is more than temporary and to a future which may be compared to the lot of the patriarch.

It was this same question of the prosperity of the wicked and the suffering of the righteous which exercised the mind of the writer of Psalm

lxxiii, and at one time seemed likely to prove fatal
to his belief in God's good Providence. The poet
tells us first of all how critical was the position of
his faith for the time being :—

But as for me, my feet were almost gone ;
My steps had well-nigh slipped.
For I was envious of the arrogant,
When I saw the prosperity of the wicked.

  And then he goes on to set forth in some detail
the position of these unrighteous men. To his
imagination they seem to escape all the ills of life
and to enjoy its good things, while all the time
they laugh God to scorn. Bitterly in conclusion
he contrasts their position with his own :—

Behold these men are ungodly,
And secure for ever, they have won great substance.
Surely in vain have I cleansed my heart,
And washed my hands in innocency ;
And yet I was plagued all the day,
And my rebuke came every morning.

  But even in his misery it comes upon him that
this is not the attitude which a member of the
true Israel ought to adopt. Such hopeless aban-
donment is in fact a denial of his belief, a proving
false to the cause of which he stands as the representative :—

If I had said, I will speak thus,
I should have been a traitor to the generation of Thy
    children.

  Therefore, when faith seems weakest, he deter-
mines to make the severest trial of faith. He

takes his difficulty into the sanctuary of God, the place which was regarded as the seat of God's earthly government, the House of prayer in which devout men were wont to see Yahwe's power and glory, and so the right spot to seek enlightenment at such a spiritual crisis. And it is here that a solution offers itself to his mind, and he meets with perfect satisfaction :—

And I kept thinking how to understand this ;
It was vain labour in my eyes :
Until I went into the sanctuary of God,
And gave heed unto their latter end.

The explanation which suggests itself to the Psalmist and satisfies his mind is not unlike that which we have seen to be put forward by the author of Psalm xxxvii. The prosperity of the wicked is, after all, more apparent than real. There is a Nemesis which is waiting in their path. Even while they stretch out their eager hands to gather life's flowers, the solid rock gives way beneath their feet, and they go down quick into the abyss :—

Surely in slippery places dost Thou set them,
Thou castest them down into ruins ;
How are they become a desolation in a moment,
Swept off, consumed by terrors !
As a dream, when one has awakened,
So Lord, when Thou arousest Thyself, Thou shalt despise
    their semblance.
O, that my heart should be embittered,
And that I should be pierced in my reins !
I indeed was brutish and ignorant.
I was like a beast before Thee.

The solution cannot be said to be final and altogether satisfactory. It represented a small advance in thought upon the old opinion ; but was in fact merely a partial and fragmentary contribution to the truth, and was destined soon to be merged in a larger view of God's dealings with men.

But this solution is not the Psalmist's real gain during his visit to the sanctuary. We find it rather in the conviction which seizes him of the great reality of his communion with God ; a conviction which calls forth from him such a confession of trust in God as forms perhaps the highest venture of faith contained in the pages of the Old Testament :—

Nevertheless, I am continually with Thee,
Thou hast holden my right hand.
According to Thy purpose wilt Thou lead me,
And afterwards wilt take me gloriously.
Whom have I in heaven ?
And, having Thee, there is naught that I desire upon
    earth ;
Though my flesh and my heart should have wasted away,
God would be the Rock of my heart and my portion
    for ever !

This passage, even more forcibly than the passage which we have already noticed in Psalm xvi. 11, illustrates the position from which the doctrine of personal immortality is really developed, viz. a strength of conviction of the reality of personal union with God, under which the thought of death as it were fades into the background and is ignored, the Psalmist feeling that he possesses all that he needs, and that, in any event, he is entirely in the hands and under the special care of his God.   Whether the Psalmist is definitely formulating his belief in a future life has been doubted ; but at any rate in the statement of verse 24[b], 'and afterward wilt take me with glory,' the expression 'afterward' seems to be contrasted with what goes before—God's support and guidance during this present life—and again we notice the expression '*wilt take me*', which, as in Psalm xlix, 15, recalls the story of Enoch— 'he was not, for God took him.'

Thus we conclude our examination of the Psalms, We have seen that they contain little or nothing which takes the shape of definitely formulated belief in a life beyond the grave, in which the anomalies of the present life will be explained and set right ; but, on the other hand, they illustrate— and that more forcibly than any other portion of the Old Testament—the height to which faith was capable of rising under the sense of communion with its God, and so they provide the fruitful soil out of which the doctrine of a personal immortality in the enjoyment of the society of God was bound sooner or later to be developed,

The Book of Job

By far the most detailed study of the problem of the suffering of the righteous is found in the Book of Job, probably a product of the age of the Exile, or a little later.   Here we find the subject treated in dramatic form, the current views as to the meaning of prosperity and adversity criticized and shown to be inadequate, and attempt made to set forward, if not a definite solution, at any rate a wider view as to the range of God's Providence which may help towards a solution.

In the Book of Job, Job represents the typical righteous man, ' perfect and upright, one that feared God and eschewed evil.' In the midst of a life of well-deserved prosperity he is suddenly overtaken by a series of extraordinary misfortunes, blow following upon blow. His three friends, who come to interview him and condole with him, represent the old standpoint that suffering, especially when so sudden and calamitous as that which has overtaken Job, must be due to sin ; and the best advice which they can offer the sufferer is to press home upon him this doctrine, to urge him to examine himself in order to discover the flagrant act of sin which has brought down upon him the hand of Yahwe with such unexampled heaviness, and to make confession and reparation of his sin. Conscious of his integrity, as regards the commission of any heinous sin, Job indignantly repudiates the charge so unjustly levelled against him. The subject is discussed in all its aspects in three cycles of speeches, in which the friends, propound their arguments and Job replies. In the third cycle, the speech of Bildad the Shuhite (ch. xxv) is extremely short, and Zophar the Naamathite fails to speak at all ; an arrangement which is perhaps intended to suggest that the friends have exhausted their arguments. The section chapters xxxii–xxxvii, in which a fourth speaker, Elihu, not mentioned in the prologue and epilogue, comes forward, is probably a later addition to the book. The section is of inferior literary style, and its insertion is detrimental to the plan of the book, in part through its repetition of the arguments of Eliphaz as to the disciplinary value of suffering, in part through anticipation of the teaching of Yahwe as to the Divine greatness. The true continuation of chapter xxxi is found in chapter xxxviii, where Yahwe answers Job out of the whirlwind. This contains the writer's main solution of the problem with which he is dealing. The greatness of God, as witnessed by inanimate and animate nature, is beyond man's comprehension. God's resources are infinite ; nothing is hid from Him, nor can be conceived as lying outside His power. It is therefore presumption on man's part to question the justice of God's rule of the world in His dealings with mankind, even though these dealings are mysterious and pass his understanding. Further points which the writer makes clear by his whole conception of Job as a righteous man who, though nearly falling under the weight of his trials, does notwithstanding maintain finally his belief in God's providence and goodness, are that there are such things as disinterested piety and undeserved sufferings. The manner in which Job, after denying the justice of God's dealings under the keen stress of his calamity, does in the end bow his head beneath the revelation of the Divine greatness and wisdom, and retract his arraignment of God's dealings with mankind, serves to emphasize the truth that suffering may be permitted by God, not as a punishment for sin, but as a discipline by means of which character is strengthened and refined.

It concerns us now to inquire whether the idea of a future life enters at all within the view of the writer as a sphere in which the moral difficulties of the present life may find their solution.

In the main, the writer is still trammelled by the old conception of the dreary half-existence in She'ol and the hopelessness of its prospect. Certain passages which illustrate this have already been noticed in the first lecture. We may add chapter vii. 9, 10 :—

As the cloud is consumed and vanisheth away,
So he that goeth down to She'ol shall come up no more.
He shall return no more to his house ;
Neither shall his place know him any more.

Especially blank and dreary is the outlook of xiv. 7–12 :—

For there is hope of a tree, if it be cut down, that it will
    sprout again,
And that the shoot thereof will not cease.
Though the root thereof wax old in the earth,
And the stock thereof die in the ground ;
Yet through the scent of water it will bud,
And put forth branches like a plant.
But man dies, and lies prostrate,

He gives up the ghost, and where is he ?
The waters fail from the sea,
And the river is parched and dries up ;
So man lies down and rises not :
Till the heavens be no more, they shall not awake,
Nor be roused out of their sleep.

While such a view of the prospect after death
holds its ground it is plain that the hope of a
future life cannot be put forward as a solution of
the writer's enigma. Yet there is a passage in
which it is suggested, as it were tentatively, only
to be immediately withdrawn as scarcely within
the range of credibility. The passage is found
in xiv. 13–15, the continuation of that last quoted,
where Job is speaking and addressing Yahwe :—

Oh that Thou wouldest hide me in She'ol,
That Thou wouldest keep me secret, until Thy wrath
    be past,
That Thou wouldest appoint me a set time and remem-
    ber me !
If a man die, shall he live again ?
All the days of my warfare would I wait,
Till my relief should come.
Thou shouldest call, and I would answer Thee.
Thou wouldest have a desire to the work of Thy hands.

In verse 14 the figure is that of a soldier at his
post, looking to the time when he shall be relieved
from his hard service. And in the following verse
Job dwells longingly upon the joy with which,
if it could indeed be anticipated, he would look
forward to the sound of Yahwe's voice, calling
him to a renewed state of fellowship with Him.

One more passage, and that, for our purpose, the most important in the book, remains to be noticed.   It is the well-known passage, chapter xix. 25–27, which certainly embodies the hope of a future life in some sense, though perhaps not precisely as it is generally understood.

Job in his misery has appealed to his friends for pity ; but they are relentless (xix. 21, 22).   They cannot abandon their principles, which compel them to regard Job as a sinner and unrepentant. Then the sufferer turns his mind to the generations yet to come, and expresses the desire that his passionate protestation of innocence might be indelibly graven in the rock, that all might read (verses 23, 24).   But here his thoughts linger but for an instant : suddenly the conviction seizes him that there is One who must ultimately vindicate his innocence in the face of the world, and that of this vindication he shall in some way gain the comfortable assurance, in spite of the near impending dissolution of his earthly frame.

The passage may be best translated thus :—

But I—I know that my Vindicator liveth,
And in after time shall take His stand upon the dust ;
And after my skin, which has been thus struck off,
Even without my flesh shall I see God.
Whom I shall see for myself,
And my eyes shall behold, and not a stranger ;
—My reins are consumed within me !

Throughout this passage the Hebrew text is somewhat difficult ; but there is little reason to doubt that it stands substantially in its original form, except in the case of the line rendered—

And after my skin, which has been thus struck off,

where the language is so harsh and the abbreviation so concise that it is impossible to place any confidence in the text, though attempt at reconstruction has totally failed, and suggested emendations are not worthy of notice. The Hebrew means literally :—

And after my skin they have struck off—this.

The verb rendered 'they have struck off' must be understood as an impersonal active in place of a passive, and the use of so strong an expression, if original, must be taken to refer to the ravages which the disease—probably elephantiasis—has made upon the sufferer. The strange 'this' at the end of the line can only be explained as used *deiktikos*. Job points to himself to illustrate the fact of which he is speaking. Hence, in accommodation to English idiom, we render 'thus'. In the succeeding line the expression which I have rendered 'without my flesh' is literally '*from*', i.e. '*away from*' or '*apart from* my flesh'. The word rendered 'Vindicator' is in Hebrew *Go'el*, properly a man's nearest blood-relation, upon whom the obligation lay to avenge his death, if he had been unjustly slain. Job pictures God as such a *Go'el*, who will surely clear him of the imputation of guilt which has been unjustly

fastened upon him. The rendering ' Redeemer '
is less suitable than ' Vindicator ', as suggesting
the idea of a Deliverer from the power of sin : a
thought which is foreign and even antagonistic
to the idea which is uppermost in the speaker's
mind. The last sentence, ' My reins are consumed
within me,' is an exclamation, as Job breaks off,
dazed by the glorious vision which he has con-
jured up before his mind's eye. The ' reins '
are in Hebrew poetry the seat of deep emotion.

This passage, then, is the highest venture of
faith contained in the book of Job. The idea of
a future life—using the expression in the sense of
an existence after death *not* wholly removed from
the presence of God—has been hinted at, as we
have seen, earlier in the book, though to the writer
it seemed beyond the reach of aspiration. Here
it bursts into expression as a conviction—something, it is true, far below the Christian ideal, as
the writer looks forward merely to a disembodied
condition—' without my flesh,' and there is no
hint that the vision of God is hoped for as a
perpetuity, or indeed as anything more than a
passing realization of the vindication by God of
the speaker's integrity. Still, it was a great
inspiration, a great venture of faith, and it forms
a step upwards in the direction of the fuller light.

III

THE PROBLEM IN THE LATER WISDOM LITERATURE

Ecclesiastes

THE work next to be examined, *Qohéleth*, 'The Preacher,' or Ecclesiastes, belongs to the later 'Wisdom' literature of the Jews.

There can be no question that Ecclesiastes, though claiming the authorship of Solomon, is really a very late production. The style of Hebrew in which the book is written, while it has numerous affinities with the later writings of the Old Testament, Chronicles, Ezra, and Nehemiah, yet exhibits many more traces of decadence, approximating in many respects to the style of the Mishna, i.e. the portion of the Talmud which was drawn up in 200 A. D.

Nor does the character of the writer suit that of Solomon as known to us. As Dr. Driver remarks,[1] 'The Solomon who speaks here is a different character from the Solomon of history. It is not Solomon the righteous judge, nor Solomon the builder of the Temple, nor even Solomon confessing his declension from a spiritual faith. There is no note of *penitence* in the entire book. Nor are the social and political allusions such as would fall from Solomon's lips. The historical Solomon,

[1] *Introduction to the Literature of the Old Testament*, p. 470.

the ruler of a great and prosperous empire, could not have penned such a satire upon his own administration as would be implied if iii. 16 (the place of judgement filled by wickedness), iv. 1 (the wrongs done by powerful oppressors), v. 8 (one corrupt ruler above another making appeal for redress useless), were written by him. The author of *Qohéleth* evinces no kingly or national feeling : he lives in a period of political servitude, destitute of patriotism or enthusiasm. When he alludes to kings, he views them from below, as one of the people suffering from their misrule. His pages reflect the depression produced by the corruption of an Oriental despotism, with its injustice (iii. 16, iv. 1, v. 8, viii. 9), its capriciousness (x. 5^f), its revolutions (x. 7), its system of spies (x. 20), its hopelessness of reform. He must have lived when the Jews had lost their national independence, and formed but a province of the Persian Empire, perhaps even later, when they had passed under the rule of the Greeks (third century B.C.). But he adopts a literary disguise, and puts his meditations into the mouth of the king, whose reputation it was to have been the great sage and philosopher of the Hebrew race, whose observation and knowledge of human nature were celebrated by tradition, and whose position might naturally be supposed to afford him the opportunity of testing systematically in his own person every form of human pursuit or enjoyment.'

The conclusion to which the writer's experience

of life has led him is tersely summed up in the oft-
repeated statement, 'Vanity of vanities; all is
vanity and the pursuit of wind.' If we look for
an advance in the conception of a future life, we
are painfully arrested. In this respect the book
falls far below the literature which we considered
in the last lecture. Life is evil, the writer thinks,
but the future beyond the grave offers no better
prospect. The best advice that can be given is
to enjoy wisely and moderately the pleasures of
life whilst they lie within reach, since failure and
disappointment are ordinarily all that the future
holds in store for man. His conception of the
state after death is the old idea of the shadowy
existence in She'ol, devoid alike of interest and
the hope of a brighter dawn. If he has heard, as
he must have done, of higher views as to man's
future, he adopts a purely agnostic position with
regard to them; in fact he refuses to see more
hope for man beyond the grave than there is for
the beast: 'That which befalleth the sons of men
befalleth beasts; even one thing befalleth them:
as the one dieth, so dieth the other; yea, they
have all one breath; and man hath no pre-
eminence above the beasts; for all is vanity. All
go unto one place; all are of the dust, and all turn
to dust again. Who knoweth the spirit of man
whether it goeth upward, and the spirit of the
beast whether it goeth downward to the earth?
Wherefore I saw that there is nothing better, than
that a man should rejoice in his works; for that

is his portion : for who shall bring him back to see
what shall be after him ? ' (iii. 19–22).   Or again :
' All things come alike to all ; there is one event
to the righteous and to the wicked ; to the good
[and to the evil],[1] to the clean and to the unclean ;
to him that sacrificeth and to him that sacrificeth
not ; as is the good, so is the sinner ; and he that
sweareth, as he that feareth an oath.   This is an
evil that is done under the sun, that there is one
event unto all : Yea also, the heart of the sons of
men is full of evil, and madness is in their heart
while they live, and after that they go to the dead.
For to him that is joined with all the living there
is hope : for a living dog is better than a dead lion.
For the living know that they shall die ; but the
dead know not anything, neither have they any
more a reward ; for the memory of them is forgotten.   As well their love, as their hatred and
their envy, is now perished ; neither have they
any more a portion for ever in anything that is
done under the sun ' (ix. 3–6).

Is there any alleviation of this blank prospect ?
There are certain passages which seem to teach
the future judgement of men in accordance with
their actions.   These are iii. 17, ' I said in my
heart, God shall judge the righteous and the
wicked :' xi. 9[b], ' But know thou, that for all these
things God will bring thee into judgement :' xii. 14,
' For God shall bring every work into judgement,
with every hidden thing, whether it be good or

[1] Supplied on the authority of the Versions.

whether it be evil.' It is, however, hard or impossible to see how such an expectation of a judgement to come, sifting the good from the bad, can have been held by the writer in conjunction with the prospect of gloomy hopelessness which we have seen to be expressed in the passages which we have noticed. There is no indication in the book that the writer is subject to alternations of hope and despair, of belief and unbelief. The work does not take the form of a debate, in which rival views are put forward, and balanced one against another. It propounds a philosophy of life which seems perfectly self-consistent; and the passages which make for another and more hopeful view are introduced abruptly and stand out in isolation from their context.

We seem therefore to be compelled, however reluctantly, to acquiesce in the opinion which regards the passages which refer to a judgement to come as later interpolations, out of harmony with the main tenor of the book.

Before leaving Ecclesiastes, we should notice that the writer, however gloomy and pessimistic his outlook may seem to be, is no agnostic as regards his belief in God, and God's government of the world. He recognizes a universal providence in the world : God is for him ' God that doeth all ' (xi. 5). The good things of life are the gifts of God, and the wisest course is to make the best of them, and enjoy them while you may. Thus iii. 12, 13, ' I know that there is nothing better

for them, than to rejoice and to get good so long
as they live. And also that every man should
eat and drink, and enjoy good in all his labour, is
the gift of God : ' v. 19, ' Every man also to whom
God hath given riches and wealth, and hath given
him power to eat thereof, and to take his portion,
and to rejoice in his labour ; this is the gift of
God : ' vii. 14, ' In the day of prosperity be joyful,
and in the day of adversity consider : God hath
even made the one side by side with the other, in
order that man should not find out what shall be
after him.' Under all circumstances the fear of
God is inculcated ; it is right to use discretion and
to know what one is doing when going to the house
of God (v. 1) ; vows when vowed must be punctu-
ally paid, for it is better not to vow at all than to
fail in performance (v. 2 ff.). The writer recognizes
the fact that the fear of God often brings its
reward, and sin its punishment : ' To the man
that pleaseth Him God giveth wisdom, and knowledge, and joy ; but to the sinner He giveth
travail, to gather and to heap up, that he may
give to him that pleaseth God ' (ii. 26). Indeed,
he can even rise to such a statement of his belief
in the Divine Providence as ' Though a sinner do
evil an hundred times, and prolong his days, yet
surely I know that it shall be well with them that
fear God, which fear before Him ; but it shall not
be well with the wicked, neither shall he prolong his
days which are as a shadow ; because he feareth
not before God ' (viii. 12, 13). Immediately, how-

ever, there follows the exception, which denies in practice the effective working out of the rule of righteousness just enunciated : ' There is a vanity which is done upon the earth ; that there be righteous men, unto whom it happeneth according to the work of the wicked ; again, there be wicked men, to whom it happeneth according to the work of the righteous : I said that this also is vanity ' (viii. 14).

In short, the author of Ecclesiastes, refusing to acknowledge any prospect of a life beyond the grave, is faced by the insoluble anomalies of the present life ; and it is these that add the gall to his cup. His philosophy of life is a mixture of Stoicism and Hedonism : life on the whole is evil, and its ills and injustices are insoluble ; but the good things of life are the gifts of God, and man's wisest course is to enjoy them while he may and to make the best of things. This is the philosophy of the Sadducees, and the writer of our book was either a member of that party, or exhibits the point of view upon which the party was shortly to be formed ; for in our ignorance of the date of the book we cannot speak with certainty. It is probable, however, that a division of schools of thought had already taken place ; and the reason why I have dwelt at some length upon the writer's religious and ethical standpoint is in order that we may notice shortly how keenly it was resented by a member of the opposite party, to whom the hope of a blessed future in store for the souls of the righteous was the climax of his religion.

Ecclesiasticus, or The Wisdom of Ben-Sira

It is convenient at this point to deal with the two examples of ' Wisdom ' literature included among the Apocrypha—Ecclesiasticus, or the Wisdom of Jesus Ben-Sira, and the Wisdom of Solomon.

The date of the Wisdom of Ben-Sira is probably to be fixed at about 180 B.C. Prior to the recent discoveries of fragments of the original Hebrew text of this work, it had been remarked by scholars that the book might be classed as ' the chief monument of early Sadduceeism', since it 'approximates to the standpoint of the primitive Ṣaduqim as regards its theology, its sacerdotalism, and its want of sympathy with the modern Soferim [or scribes]. The name of *Ezra* is significantly omitted from its catalogue of worthies'. It was interesting, therefore, to discover at the end of the Hebrew text of the book a hymn, previously unknown, which ends with praise of the sons of Zadok :—

O give thanks unto Him that maketh to bud a horn for
    the house of David ;
For His mercy endureth for ever.
O give thanks unto Him that chose the sons of Zadok
    to be priests ;
For His mercy endureth for ever.

As a Sadducee, the writer offers no advance upon the teaching of Ecclesiastes with regard to the existence after death, though he by no means shares the pessimistic outlook of the latter writer with regard to life in general. His view of death is that of a man of the world who sees no hope in the hereafter :—

My son, let thy tears fall over the dead,
And as one that suffereth grievously begin lamentation ;
And wind up his body according to his due,
And neglect not his burial.
Make bitter weeping, and make passionate wailing,
And let thy mourning be according to his desert,
For one day or two, lest thou be evil spoken of :
And so be comforted for thy sorrow,
For of sorrow cometh death,
And sorrow of heart will bow down the strength.
In calamity sorrow also remaineth :
And the poor man's life is grievous to the heart.
Give not thy heart unto sorrow ;
Put it away, remembering the last end :
Forget it not, for there is no returning again :
Him thou shalt not profit, and thou wilt hurt thyself.
Remember the sentence upon him ; for so also shall
    thine be ;
Yesterday for me, and to-day for thee.
When the dead is at rest, let his remembrance rest ;
And be comforted for him, when his spirit departeth
    from him.—xxxviii. 16–23.

In another passage he apostrophizes Death :—

O Death, how bitter is the remembrance of thee to a man
    that is at peace in his possessions,
Unto the man that hath nothing to distract him, and
    hath prosperity in all things,
And that still hath strength to receive meat !
O Death, acceptable is thy sentence unto a man that is
    needy, and that faileth in strength,
That is in extreme old age, and is distracted about all
    things,

And is perverse, and hath lost patience !
Fear not the sentence of death ;
Remember them that have been before thee, and that
    come after :
This is the sentence from the Lord over all flesh.
And why dost thou refuse, when it is the good pleasure
    of the Most High ?
Whether it be ten, or a hundred, or a thousand years,
There is no inquisition of life in She'ol.—xli. 1–4.

His advice, like that of the writer of Ecclesiastes,
is to make the most of the present life, in view of
the approach of death which is inevitable :—

My son, according as thou hast, do well unto thy self,
And bring offerings unto the Lord worthily.
Remember that Death will not tarry,
And that the covenant of She'ol is not showed unto
    thee.
Do well unto thy friend before thou die ;
And according to thy ability stretch out thy hand and
    give to him.
Defraud not thyself of a good day ;
And let not the portion of a good desire pass thee by.
Shalt thou not leave thy labours unto another ?
And thy toils to be divided by lot ?
Give and take, and beguile thy soul ;
For there is no seeking of luxury in She'ol.
All flesh waxeth old as a garment ;
For the covenant from the beginning is,
Thou shalt die the death.—xiv. 11–17.

Ben-Sira's view that there is no praise of God in
She'ol reminds us of the sentiment expressed in
the song of Hezekiah, and in some of the Psalms :—

Who shall give praise to the Most High in She'ol,
Instead of them that live and return thanks ?

Thanksgiving perisheth from the dead, as from one that
   is not :
He that is in life and health shall praise the Lord.
                                        —xvii. 27, 28.

There are passages in which death seems to be
regarded as an eternal sleep.   Thus in xlvi. 19
Samuel's death is spoken of as ' his long sleep ' ;
xxx. 17 says that—

> Death is better than a bitter life,
> And eternal rest than a continual sickness ;

xxii. 11 says of the dead that ' he hath found rest ' ;
and the same statement is made in xxxviii. 23.

   Such being the writer's views with regard to
death, it is surprising to read in vii. 17 that—

The punishment of the ungodly man is fire and the worm,

a statement which presupposes belief in a penal
Gehenna for the wicked.   Such a belief is in direct
contradiction to the assertion of xli. 4 that—

> There is no inquisition of life in She'ol.

Reference, however, to the original Hebrew text,
in which this passage happens to be preserved,
shows us that the line originally ran—

> For the expectation of man is the worm,

giving the reason for the injunction of the preceding
line,

> Humble thy soul very exceedingly,

and referring merely to the destruction of the body
through corruption as a motive for humility.   The
passage in the Greek must have undergone later
alteration, in order to introduce the idea of future

punishment for the wicked, contrary to the opinion of Ben-Sira.

It is remárkable, however, how more than once the writer lays stress upon the importance of a good death in language which, taken out of its context, might be supposed to imply a belief in the recompense of a future life. Thus in i. 13 he says :—

Whoso feareth the Lord, it shall go well with him at the last,
And in the day of his death he shall be blessed.

So in vii. 36 :—

In all thy matters remember thy last end,
And thou shalt never do amiss.

And again in xi. 26–28 :—

For it is an easy thing in the sight of the Lord
To reward a man in the day of death according to his ways.
The affliction of an hour causeth forgetfulness of delight ;
And in the last end of a man is the revelation of his deeds.
Call no man blessed before his death ;
And a man shall be known in his children.

The reason is that Ben-Sira regards *a good name*, or, as we should say, an untarnished reputation, as the highest ideal after which a man can strive. If he can leave such a name behind him, he has secured some sort of immortality upon earth ; but the possession of such a name is not secure until the day of death ; hence the importance of a good death-bed.

The writer's opinion of the value of a good

name may be illustrated by the following passages :—

The wise man shall inherit confidence among his people,
And his name shall live for ever.—xxxvii. 26.

Have regard to thy name ;
For it continueth with thee longer than a thousand great
     treasures of gold.
A good life hath its number of days ;
But a good name continueth for ever.—xli. 12, 13.

A good man has also a reward for his righteousness in *his children*, who carry on his reputation and so help to secure the immortality of his name. Thus :—

A man shall be known through his children.—xi. 28.
Children and the building of a city establish a man's name.
                         —xl. 19.

The worthies of the past possess a kind of immortality in their *name* and in their *posterity* :—

But these were men of mercy,
Whose righteous deeds have not been forgotten.
With their seed shall remain continually a good inherit-
     ance ;
Their children are within the covenants,
Their seed standeth fast,
And their children for their sakes.
Their seed shall remain for ever,
And their glory shall not be blotted out.
Their bodies were buried in peace,
And their name liveth to all generations.
People will declare their wisdom,
And the congregation telleth out their praise.
                         —xliv. 10–15.

The wicked, on the other hand, if not punished in

this life, are punished eventually through the evil reputation of their 'name', and through the misfortunes of their children. Thus, of the unfaithful wife, it is stated that—

Her children shall not spread into roots,
And her branches shall bear no fruit.
She shall leave her memory for a curse ;
And her reproach shall not be blotted out.
And they that are left behind shall know that there is
     nothing better than the fear of the Lord,
And nothing sweeter than to take heed to the command-
     ments of the Lord.—xxiii. 25–27.

xl. 15 asserts that—

The children of the ungodly shall not put forth many
     branches ;
And are as unclean roots upon a sheer rock.

In xli. 5–7 we read :—

The children of sinners are abominable children,
And they frequent the dwellings of the ungodly.
The inheritance of sinners' children shall perish,
And with their posterity shall be a perpetual reproach.
Children will complain of an ungodly father,
Because they shall be reproached for his sake.

Thus, according to Ben-Sira, righteousness and wickedness, if not recompensed during a man's lifetime, meet their reward ultimately through the reputation after death, and through the character and fortunes of descendants.

The refining value of suffering to the righteous, and the sure fact of God's righteous dealing

towards them, are asserted in as fine a passage as
is contained in the book :—

My son, if thou comest to serve the Lord,
Prepare thy soul for temptation.
Set thy heart aright and constantly endure,
And make not haste in time of calamity.
Cleave unto Him, and depart not,
That thou mayst be increased at thy latter end.
Accept whatsoever is brought upon thee,
And be patient when thou passest into humiliation.
For gold is tried in the fire,
And acceptable men in the furnace of humiliation.
Put thy trust in Him : and He will help thee :
Order thy ways aright and set thy hope on Him.
Ye that fear the Lord, wait for His mercy ;
And turn not aside, lest ye fall.
Ye that fear the Lord, put your trust in Him ;
And your reward shall not fail.
Ye that fear the Lord, hope for good things,
And for eternal gladness and mercy.
Look at the generations of old, and see :
Who did ever put his trust in the Lord, and was ashamed ?
Or who did abide in His fear, and was forsaken ?
Or who did call upon Him, and He despised him ?
For the Lord is full of compassion and mercy ;
And He forgiveth sins, and saveth in time of affliction.
—ii. 1-11.

The Wisdom of Solomon

The Book of the Wisdom of Solomon gains its
title from the fact that the author, like the author
of Ecclesiastes, puts his sentiments into the mouth
of Solomon, the founder of proverbial wisdom.
We may notice vii. 5, and especially ix. 7, 8. As
to the date of the book there is no consensus of

opinion ; but few scholars are inclined to date it earlier than 100 B.C., and some would place it as late as 40 A.D. That the author was an Alexandrine Jew is clear from his acquaintance with Egyptian religion, and might also be inferred from the fact that he has received an education in Greek philosophy, and inclines in some respects to Platonic conceptions, e.g. the eternity of matter (xi. 17), and the pre-existence of the soul (viii. 19, 20). As regards the doctrine of a future life he stands out in salient contrast to the two writers whom we have just been considering, for his insistence upon individual immortality is the most prominent characteristic of his teaching. His antagonism to such a view of life as is put forward by Ecclesiastes is very marked : it even seems possible that he may have employed the name of Solomon as the exponent of the true Wisdom as against the use of the name by Ecclesiastes ; and the terms in which he describes the philosophy of life adopted by the ' ungodly' read almost like an abstract of the contents of Ecclesiastes as interpreted by a hostile critic :—

God made not death ;
Neither delighteth He when the living perish :
For He created all things that they might have being :
And the generative powers of the world are healthsome,
And there is no poison of destruction in them :
Nor hath Hades royal dominion upon earth.
For righteousness is immortal :
But ungodly men by their hands and their words called
    Hades unto them :

Deeming him a friend they consumed away,
And they made a covenant with him,
Because they are worthy to be his portion.
For they said within themselves, reasoning not aright,
Short and sorrowful is our life ;
And there is no healing when a man cometh to his end,
And none was ever known that gave release from Hades.
Because by mere chance were we born,
And hereafter we shall be as though we had never been
Because the breath of our nostrils is smoke,
And reason is a spark kindled by the beating of our heart,
Which being extinguished, the body shall be turned into
    ashes,
And the spirit shall be dispersed as thin air ;
And our name shall be forgotten in time,
And no man shall remember our works ;
And our life shall pass away as the traces of a cloud,
And shall be scattered as is a mist,
When it is chased by the beams of the sun,
And overcome by the heat thereof.
For our allotted time is the passing of a shadow,
And there is no putting back of our end ;
Because it is fast sealed, and none turneth it back.
Come therefore and let us enjoy the good things that
    now are ;
And let us use the creation with all our soul as youth's
    possession.
Let us fill ourselves with costly wine and perfumes ;
And let no flower of spring pass us by :
Let us crown ourselves with rosebuds, before they be
    withered :
Let none of us go without his share in our proud revelry :
Everywhere let us leave tokens of our mirth :
Because this is our portion, and our lot is this.

—i. 13—ii. 9.

This Epicurean view of life, the writer states,
goes hand in hand with oppression and persecu-

tion of the righteous, whose standard of life appears
as an open reproof to the ungodly, and whom they
therefore desire to condemn to a shameful death.
So doing, they fail to realize that they can have
no real hold over the godly man, for—

They knew not the mysteries of God,
Neither hoped they for wages of holiness,
Nor did they judge that there is a prize for blameless
    souls.
Because God created man for incorruption,
And made him an image of His own proper being ;
But by the envy of the devil death entered into the
    world.
And they that are his portion make trial thereof.

—ii. 22–24.

And then follows the well-known passage in which
the writer develops his theme as to the blessed
future in store for the righteous :—

But the souls of the righteous are in the hand of God,
And no torment shall touch them.
In the eyes of the foolish they seemed to have died :
And their departure was accounted to be their hurt,
And their journeying away from us to be their ruin :
But they are in peace.
For even if in the sight of men they be punished,
Their hope is full of immortality ;
And having borne a little chastening, they shall receive
    great good ;
Because God made trial of them, and found them worthy
    of Himself.
As gold in the furnace He proved them,
And as a whole burnt-offering He accepted them.
And in the time of their visitation they shall shine
    forth,

And as sparks among stubble they shall run to and fro.
They shall judge nations, and have dominion over peoples;
And the Lord shall reign over them for evermore.
They that trust on Him shall understand truth.
And the faithful shall abide with Him in love ;
Because grace and mercy are to His chosen.—iii. 1–9.

Precisely what form the immortality of the righteous dead is to take is not made very clear by the writer. According to Dr. Charles,[1] the writer's view is that ' there will be no resurrection of the body ; for the soul is the proper self : the body is a mere burden taken up by the pre-existent soul, but in due season laid down again. Accordingly, there is only an immortality of the soul '.

It is hard to believe in the correctness of this verdict in view of the passage which I have just quoted. It is acknowledged that the writer looks forward to ' the Messianic or Theocratic kingdom, where the righteous will judge the nations and have dominion '. But apparently, in Dr. Charles's opinion, these righteous are not the faithful departed, but those who live on until the establishment of the kingdom upon earth. Such a view, however, is inconceivable. The whole passage, iii. 1–9, is speaking of the same people. The righteous who ' seemed to have died ', whose ' departure was accounted to be their hurt, and their journeying away from us to be their ruin ', are the same who ' shall judge nations, and have dominion over peoples ', this being part of ' their

---

[1] Hastings, *Bible Dictionary*, i. 746.

hope' which 'is full of immortality'. So much
would be clear from the passage if it stood by itself.
But it is increasingly clear when the writer's
dependence upon the Book of Daniel is recognized.
The writer has in mind Daniel vii. 18 : ' The saints
of the Most High shall receive the kingdom, and
possess the kingdom for ever, even for ever and
ever,' and verse 22, ' Judgement was given to the
saints of the Most High ; and the time came that
the saints possessed the kingdom.' This is clear
from Wisdom iii. 7ᵃ :—

In the time of their visitation they shall shine forth,

which can hardly be anything else than a reminis-
cence of Daniel xii. 3, ' They that be wise shall
shine forth as the brightness of the firmament.'

Thus the 'time of their visitation' refers to the
event of Daniel xii. 1, when Michael shall stand up
and after a period of great trouble the righteous
Israel is to be delivered and ' many of them that
sleep in the land of dust shall awake '. It is the
righteous among these that ' shall shine forth as
the brightness of the firmament ' ; and these are
identical with the righteous of whom the author
of Wisdom is speaking.

We may conclude, then, that the author of
Wisdom looks forward to a theocratic kingdom,
apparently to be established upon earth, in which
the saints are to have dominion. These saints
probably include those who survive to the time of
the establishment of the kingdom, but also cer-

tainly the blessed dead who are to be raised so as
to have their part in the kingdom, and therefore,
it may be assumed, to be raised *with* their
bodies.

Time will not admit of our entering in detail
into the writer's conception of the judgement and
retribution of the righteous and wicked. We must
notice, however, that with the establishment of
the doctrine of a blessed immortality for the
righteous, there disappears the old idea that long
life on earth is necessarily a mark of Divine
favour, and a short life to be regarded as the lot
of the wicked.

The writer's views on the subject are expressed
in the following passage :—

But a righteous man, though he die before his time,
  shall be at rest.
(For honourable old age is not that which standeth in
  length of time,
Nor is its measure given by number of years ;
But understanding is grey hairs unto men,
And an unspotted life is ripe old age.)
Being found well pleasing unto God he was beloved of
  Him,
And while living among sinners he was translated :
He was caught away lest wickedness should change his
  understanding,
Or guile deceive his soul.

. . . .

Being made perfect in a little while, he fulfilled long
  years ;
For his soul was pleasing unto the Lord :
Therefore hasted he out of the midst of wickedness.

—iv. 7–14.

The final judgement scene, when the wicked

Shall come, when their sins are reckoned up with coward
　　fear ;
And their lawless deeds shall convict them to their face ;

but, on the other hand—

　　The righteous man shall stand in great boldness
　　Before the face of them that afflicted him,

is depicted in a dramatic passage of great beauty
in chapter iv. 20 and chapter v.

In comparing the views of this writer as to individual immortality with anything which we have
noticed in the literature with which we have
already dealt, we are at once struck with the
contrast. In the earlier literature which we have
examined the idea of immortality appears at best
as a conviction of individual souls, or a hope
which is nothing more than a hope, almost beyond
the reach of aspiration. In Wisdom, on the
contrary, it appears, we may say, as a developed
dogma ; at any rate it is the goal of the writer's
religious aspirations, not merely for himself as an
individual, but for the elect among his nation.
This doctrine of immortality, too, is associated
with the expectation of a coming theocratic
kingdom, when the righteous

Shall judge nations, and have dominion over peoples ;
And the Lord shall reign over them for evermore.

There is, then, a great gap between the conception of the writer of Wisdom, and such conceptions
as we have found in the other literature which we

have considered. We have really dealt with the Book of Wisdom out of its place, and have associated it for convenience' sake with the other examples of Wisdom literature, Ecclesiastes, and the Wisdom of Ben-Sira.

The gap in thought which we have noticed is bridged by the important class of Jewish literature which is known as Apocalyptic. Our next task, therefore, is to pass to consideration of the manner in which the doctrine of a future life is developed in Apocalyptic literature.

IV

The Apocalyptic Literature

THE last lecture brought us up to the point at which it becomes necessary to consider the Apocalyptic literature of Judaism, in order to gain an idea of the contribution made by this literature to the doctrine of a future life.

As a preliminary it is well to understand what is included under the title ' Apocalyptic '.[1]

Speaking of this literature generally, it may be noticed in the first place that it is the product of an age of great suffering for the faithful servants of Yahwe. As a matter of fact, it first comes into evidence most markedly in the early middle part of the second century B. C., which witnessed the sufferings and persecutions of the faithful under Antiochus Epiphanes, and the rise of the Maccabaean patriots.

It should further be noticed that Apocalyptic is the product of an age when prophecy had ceased. The lack of any one who could claim the title of prophet of Yahwe is noticed several times in I Maccabees. So in iv. 46 in the account of the

---

[1] In the summary of the characteristics of Apocalyptic and the sketch of the Enoch literature contained in this article, the writer wishes to acknowledge the debt which he owes to Dr. Charles, whose works are indispensable to students of this branch of Jewish literature.

restoration of the Temple by Judas Maccabaeus
after its desecration, it is related that 'they pulled
down the altar' which had been defiled by the
Gentiles, 'and laid up the stones in the mountain
of the house in a convenient place, until there
should come a prophet to give an answer concern-
ing them.' Again, ix. 27 states that, after the
death of Judas, 'there was great tribulation in
Israel, such as was not since the time that no
prophet appeared unto them.' And, once more,
xiv. 41 relates that 'the Jews and the priests were
well pleased that Simon should be their leader and
high-priest for ever, until there should arise a
faithful prophet'.

A Maccabaean Psalm, lxxiv. 9, deplores this fact
of the absence of prophecy :—

We see not our signs ;
There is no more any prophet ;
Neither is there any among us that knoweth how long.
Yahwe, how long shall the adversary reproach ?
Shall the enemy blaspheme Thy name for ever ?

Apocalyptic, then, was designed as an answer to
this cry of the suffering faithful, 'how long?'
Let us notice the points in which it differs from
prophecy, and the characteristics of its method.

Firstly, prophecy is designed, at least in the
first place, to meet the needs of the age at which
it was spoken. It still sees hope in the present,
and it addresses itself to the men of its day with
the message 'Thus saith Yahwe', rebuking and
warning, exhorting and promising. As Dr. Charles

has put it, ' Prophecy still believes that this world is God's world, and that in this world His goodness and truth will yet be justified.' Apocalyptic, on the other hand, ' almost wholly despairs of the present.' The world appears too bad, the times too wretched, for the seed of goodness still to take root. It is no use, in the writer's opinion, to address words of warning and exhortation to his contemporaries ; the time is past when they might have heard, and returned to Yahwe. His message, therefore, is only to the elect, the small body of faithful men in the midst of a wicked world who are sore tried and need encouragement as to the limit and issue of their sufferings. As a condition of success, it was necessary for the writer of Apocalyptic to conceal his identity, and to give to his work the form of a revelation or Apocalypse made in the past to some great one, such as Enoch or Moses, Isaiah or Daniel. The course of history up to the time of the actual writer thus takes the form of a prediction made to the assumed author, though actually it is of course nothing more than a review of the past. Actual prediction comes in in the account of the turn which events are to take in the consummation and issue of the age of suffering for which the work is written. I need scarcely remark that we must not judge of the Apocalyptic writer's honesty by the standard of the present day, but must regard his method as a product of the peculiar stress and difficulty of the times in which he lived.

Another difference between prophecy and Apocalyptic is that, whereas prophecy is usually limited in its immediate scope, having to do with the people and circumstances of a particular age, Apocalyptic takes ' an indefinitely wider view of the world's history '. This is because it dates from a time when the chosen people had come under the sway of one or other of the great world-powers, and therefore the writer, in his review of the past, which he represents as future, has to take account of the part played by these great powers in the counsel of God. The final issue, too, to which he is leading up is the judgement of the world, when the saints shall possess the kingdom, a kingdom not of this world, but supramundane in its main characteristics.

Further, it must be noticed that Apocalyptic, in its prediction of the final period which is still future to the actual writer, i. e. which lies beyond the age of suffering for which he writes, builds largely upon past prophecies which were taken to be still unfulfilled, often literalizing symbolic language, and allegorizing statements of fact. This tendency to take up unfulfilled prophecy and to readapt it appears as far back as the Exile, in the prophet Ezekiel who has been described as the spiritual father of Apocalyptic.[1] Thus Jeremiah and Zephaniah had predicted the invasion of Judah by a foe from the North. This had not taken place. So Ezekiel takes up the

[1] Duhm, *Theologie der Propheten*, p. 210.

prediction (in xxxviii. 8–16), and applies it to the
advent of the host of Gog which will in the future
attack Jerusalem from the North. In the same
way Jeremiah's promise (xxv. 11 ; xxix. 10) that
after seventy years Israel should be restored to
their own land and that the Messianic age should
then supervene, is interpreted by the author of
Daniel as meaning seventy weeks of years, i.e.
490 years. Sixty-nine and a half of these weeks
having elapsed, according to this writer, there
remained only half a week, i.e. three and a half
years, before the consummation of the promise and
the advent of the Messianic kingdom.

Other instances of this new application of old
prophecies we shall notice later. What particularly concerns us is that certain of the prophets
speak of the restoration of the nation under the
figure of a resurrection. Thus we may notice the
passage in Hosea vi. 1, 2 : ' Come and let us
return unto Yahwe : for He hath torn, and He
will heal us ; He hath smitten, and He will bind
us up. After two days He will revive us : on the
third day He will raise us up, and we shall live
before him.' Similarly, in Ezekiel xxxvii, the
vision of the resuscitation of the dry bones is
figurative of the national restoration : ' Son of
man, these bones are the whole house of Israel :
behold, they say, Our bones are dried up, and
our hope is lost ; we are clean cut off. Therefore
prophesy, and say unto them, Thus saith Yahwe
Elohim : Behold, I will open your graves, and

cause you to come up out of your graves, O My people ; and I will bring you unto the land of Israel. And ye shall know that I am Yahwe, when I have opened your graves, and caused you to come up out of your graves, O My people. And I will put My spirit in you, and ye shall live, and I will place you in your own land : and ye shall know that I Yahwe have spoken it, and performed it, saith Yahwe ' (verses 11–14). And, again, in the exilic prophecy of Isaiah liii the vicarious sufferings and final restoration of the ideal Israel are pictured under the figure of the death and resurrection of the Servant of Yahwe : ' Yet it pleased Yahwe to bruise Him, and that sorely : when His soul shall make an offering for sin, He shall see His seed, He shall prolong His days, and the pleasure of Yahwe shall prosper in His hand. After the travail of His soul He shall see and be satisfied ; by His knowledge shall My righteous servant make many righteous : and He shall bear their iniquities. Therefore will I divide Him a portion with the great, and with the mighty shall He divide the spoil ; because He poured out His soul unto death, and with transgressors He let Himself be numbered, and 'twas He who bare the sins of many, and made intercession for the transgressors ' (verses 10–12).

These prophecies of the resurrection of the nation, doubtless intended in the first place as figures, appear to have been taken up and literalized in Apocalyptic, and to have formed the basis of the idea, which soon becomes a dogma, of the resurrection of the elect.

The first example of Apocalyptic which we must notice really holds as it were an intermediate place between prophecy and Apocalyptic. It is found incorporated in the Book of Isaiah as chapters xxiv–xxvii. I need not here pause to argue the non-Isaianic authorship of this section. It has to do, not with the affairs of Judah and Assyria in the eighth century B. C., but with the final judgement of the world. The characteristics of Apocalyptic are there in the world-wide outlook and the hopeless condition of the present age.

There is little or nothing by which to date the composition. The whole earth is pictured as withering under a curse. In xxiv. 10–12 there is allusion to a great city, but it is unnamed. Various suggestions have been offered as to the historical background, e. g. ' the age immediately succeeding the Exile, particularly the Babylonian troubles under Darius Hystaspis ; ' or ' the events which preceded the dissolution of the Persian Empire (say B. C. 350–330) ' ; or ' the reign of John Hyrcanus ' with ' allusions to the Parthian campaign of Antiochus Sidetes (B. C. 129) and the destruction of Samaria (cir. 107) '.[1]

The idea of a resurrection of the faithful Israelites who have been deprived by death of their share in the national restoration is introduced with almost startling suddenness in xxvi. 19. The

[1] Cf. Skinner, *Isaiah* (*Camb. Bible*), vol. i, p. 204.

previous verses lament the incapacity of the nation
to produce sufficient population to people the
world, under the figure of a woman labouring
ineffectually to bring forth. The Divine response
is, ' Thy dead shall live, My dead bodies shall
arise ; awake and shout for joy, ye dwellers in
the dust, for a dew of lights is thy dew, and the
earth shall bring forth shades.' The resurrection
here pictured is confined to the elect of the nation,
but is expressly denied in the case of their foes
in verse 14 : ' They are dead, they shall not live,
they are shades, they shall not arise ; therefore
hast Thou visited and destroyed them, and hast
made all their memorial to perish.'

This passage, then, is of peculiar interest as
being probably the earliest prediction of a general
resurrection of the elect of Israel.

In the Book of Daniel we pass to Apocalyptic
properly so called. There can be no doubt that
the book was composed during the persecution
of Antiochus Epiphanes in B. C. 168 or 167. Like
other examples of Apocalyptic it is the work of
some member of the class who remained faithful
to the religion of Yahwe in face of the efforts
which were made to complete the Hellenization
of the Jews. This class was known as the *Chasîdim*
or ' saintly ones ', a name which appears in Greek
form as Asidaeans. The Chasîdim ultimately became known as the Pĕrûshim, ' separatists ' or
Pharisees, a sect which, whatever its degeneracy,
as a whole or more probably in part, in the time

of our Lord, was in earlier times the representative of all that was best and most vigorous in the religious life of the nation.

The writer of Daniel looks forward, after the destruction of the last great world-kingdom, to a time when ' the kingdom and the dominion, and the greatness of the kingdoms under the whole heaven, shall be given to the people of the saints of the Most High : His kingdom is an everlasting kingdom, and all dominions shall serve and obey Him ' (vii. 27). In the final chapter the deliverance of the nation is confined to the elect, ' every one that shall be found written in the book,' i.e. at the final scene when ' the judgement is set and the books are opened '. The writer goes on to state that ' Many of them that sleep in the land of dust shall awake, some to everlasting life, and some to reproaches and everlasting abhorrence. And they that be wise shall shine forth as the brightness of the firmament ; and they that make many righteous as the stars for ever and ever ' (xii. 2, 3). Here we have the resurrection extended to the wicked as well as to the righteous, though here again it seems not to be pictured as general, since it speaks of ' many ' and not ' all '.

This passage has its root in earlier prophecies. The expression ' they that make many righteous ' is in Hebrew nearly identical with the expression used in Isaiah liii. 11 of the suffering Servant of Yahwe : ' Through His knowledge shall My righteous servant make many righteous,' and there can

be no doubt that there is allusion to this passage.
It is interesting, therefore, to find that so early
as this the prophecy of the Servant of Yahwe
was interpreted as referring to the righteous
nucleus of the nation.   The statement ' some to
shame and everlasting abhorrence ' goes back to
the last verse of the last chapter of Isaiah (lxvi. 24),
a passage which pictures the destruction of the
unfaithful members of the nation outside of
Jerusalem, and states that, when ' all flesh ' shall
come and worship Yahwe at Jerusalem, ' they
shall go forth and look upon the carcases of the
men who have transgressed against Me, for their
worm dieth not and their fire is not quenched ;
and they shall be an abhorrence to all flesh.'
Reference to this passage is certified by the use
both in Isaiah and Daniel of the peculiar word
for ' abhorrence ', דֵּרָאוֹן, which occurs nowhere
else throughout the Old Testament.   It appears
that the site upon which these unburied corpses
are pictured as lying was localized by later thought
in the valley of Hinnom, in Hebrew גֵּי חִנֹּם, which
appears in Greek form γέεννα, the place which in
old time was connected with the fires of the human
sacrifices to Moloch, and which later on became a
receptacle for refuse.   Here, then, we trace the
origin of the conception of Gehenna as a place
of torment for the wicked in the state beyond
the grave.

In the short space still at our disposal it would
be impossible to deal, even cursorily, with Jewish

Apocalyptic as a whole. I propose, therefore, to take the Book of Enoch, as the most interesting example of this class of literature outside the Old Testament, and to consider the development of the conception of a future life as therein contained.

The name of the Book of Enoch is familiar from the fact that it is quoted in the Epistle of St. Jude, verses 14, 15 : ' And Enoch also, the seventh from Adam, prophesied of these men, saying, Behold, the Lord cometh with ten thousands of His holy ones to execute judgement on all, and to convict all the impious of all the works of impiety which they have impiously committed, and of all the harsh sayings which impious sinners have spoken against Him.' There can be no doubt that the Book of Enoch was familiar to our Lord and to the New Testament writers, many traces of its thought and diction occurring throughout the New Testament.

In speaking of the *Book* of Enoch we are referring to the work as known to us in an Ethiopic version which was made from the Greek, which itself went back doubtless to a Hebrew original. But there can be no doubt that the *Book* as known to us represents, not a single work, but a *literature*. This may be gathered from the different views and standpoints of different sections of the work. The Old Testament statement with regard to Enoch, that he ' walked with God ', was interpreted to mean, not merely that he led an upright and godly life, but that he was the recipient of special revelations with regard to the future. Hence the name of Enoch became a favourite name with which to associate Apocalyptic, and there grew up in the second and first centuries B. C. an Enoch-literature, examples of which we have preserved for us in the Ethiopic Book of Enoch.

In distinguishing the different sections of the Book of Enoch I shall follow Dr. Charles in his edition of the book and in his work on *Eschatology*.

The first section consists of chapters i–xxxvi, ' written at latest before B. C. 170.'

Section II is formed by chapters lxxxiii–xc, ' written between B. C. 166–161.'

Section III consists of chapters xci–xciv, ' written between B. C. 134–94, or possibly B. C. 104–94.'

Section IV, containing the Similitudes, runs from chapter xxxvii to chapter lxx, and was ' written between B. C. 94–79 or B. C. 70–64 '.

Section V, the Book of Celestial Physics, consists of chapters lxxii–lxxviii, lxxxii, lxxix. This section offers no clue as to its date, and contains nothing which concerns our special purpose.

Besides these five sections, there are various interpolations from an Apocalypse of Noah, which need not here concern us.

Section I, i. e. chapters i–xxxvi, is dated before B.C. 170 mainly because it contains no sort of reference to the persecutions of Antiochus Epiphanes. It is therefore earlier than the Book of Daniel, in which, as we have noticed, the persecutions are presupposed.

This section opens with allusion to the fact that the reward of the righteous and the punishment of the wicked, though deferred, must ultimately come to pass : ' The words of the blessing of Enoch, wherewith he blessed the elect and righteous, who will be living in the day of tribulation, when all the wicked and godless are to be removed.' A great world-judgement must ultimately come to pass when all men shall be judged by God in accordance with their works. ' But to the righteous He will give peace and will protect the elect, and grace will be upon them, and they will all belong to God, and it will be well with them, and they will be blessed, and the light of God will shine upon them.' The origin of sin in the world is traced to the sin of the fallen angels, as narrated in Genesis vi. 1-4. On account of this sin the angels were confined in caverns under the mountains as an intermediate place of punishment, and the souls of men were doomed to She'ol. The fresh outbreak of sin in the world after the Deluge is traced to the agency of the spirits of the offspring of the sons of God and daughters of men, who are allowed to exercise activity in the world as demons until the final judgement.

The writer's conception of She'ol is given in great detail in chapter xxii, which narrates how

OF IMMORTALITY 91

Enoch is shown the place by the holy angels :
' And thence I went to another place, and (Uriel)
showed me in the west a great and high mountain
and hard rocks. And there were in this (mountain) four hollow places, deep, wide and very
smooth. Three of them were gloomy and one
bright, and there was a spring of water in its
midst. And I said : How smooth are these
hollow places, and deep and black to look at.
And this time Rufael answered me, one of the
holy angels who was with me, and spake to me :
These hollow places, whereon the spirits of the
souls of the dead are assembled, have been created
to this very end, that all the souls of the children
of men should assemble there. These places are
appointed as their habitation till the day of their
judgement, and till their appointed period, and
the appointed time in which the great judgement
comes upon them. And I saw the spirits of the
children of men who were dead, and their voice
penetrated to the heaven and complained. This
time I asked the angel Rufael who was with me,
and spake to him : Whose spirit is that one
yonder whose voice thus penetrates (to heaven)
and complains ? And he answered me, and spake
thus to me, saying : This is the spirit which went
forth from Abel, whom his brother Cain slew, and he
keeps complaining of him till his seed is destroyed
from the face of the earth, and his seed disappears
from amongst the seed of men. And therefore
at that time I asked regarding it, and regarding

the hollow places, Why is one separated from the other ? And he answered me, and spake to me : These three divisions are made to separate the spirits of the dead. And thus a division is made for the spirits of the righteous, in which there is a bright spring of water. Such a (division) likewise has been made for sinners when they die and are buried in the earth without incurring judgement in their lifetime. Here their spirits are placed apart in this great pain, till the great day of judgement and punishment and torment of the accursed for ever, and vengeance for their spirits, there will they be bound for ever. And such a division has been made for the spirits of those who complain and make known their destruction when they were slain in the day of the sinners. Thus it has been made for the spirits of men who were not righteous but sinners, complete in their crimes : they will be with 'criminals like themselves, but their spirits will not be slain in the day of judgement, nor will they be raised from thence.'

Here we find a conception of She'ol as divided into four divisions : two for the righteous and two for the wicked. The righteous who have been unjustly slain by the wicked complain to God and cry aloud for vengeance. Here we probably have the origin of the passage in Revelation vi. 9, 10 which speaks of the spirits of the martyrs as dwelling beneath the altar, and calling upon God to avenge their blood. The second division, con-

sisting of the other righteous, inhabit a region
which is to all intents the Paradise of later conceptions. The first of the two divisions allotted
to the wicked is inhabited by those wicked who
have not met with punishment during their
earthly life. These wicked, who already suffer
great pain in their intermediate abode, are destined
to be raised together with the two divisions of the
righteous at the judgement-day, and to receive
their final sentence. The second division of the
wicked, as having already received punishment
on earth, will not be raised to meet their doom
at the day of judgement, but are destined to
remain in She'ol for ever.

After the judgement there is to ensue for the
righteous an age of bliss and happiness on earth,
the conception of which is framed upon the lines
of the Messianic age as pictured by the prophets.
In this Messianic Kingdom there is no earthly
Messiah, his place being taken by the immediate
presence of God 'the eternal King' (xxv. 1).
The future prosperity of the righteous is conceived upon somewhat sensuous lines. The righteous will beget 1000 children (x. 17) : and the
produce of the soil will exhibit marvellous fertility
(x. 19). Emphasis is, however, also laid upon
the moral aspects of the future bliss : 'for the
elect there will be wisdom, joy, and peace, and
they will inherit the earth. . . . Then too will
wisdom be bestowed upon the elect, and they
will all live and never again sin, either through

heedlessness or through pride, but they who are wise will be humble nor fall again into sin ' (v. 7, 8). ' All the children of men shall become righteous, and all nations shall offer [God] adoration and praise, and all will worship Him ' (x. 21).

The wicked, on the other hand, i.e. the class who were not punished on earth, and whose souls are therefore raised at the judgement-day, are condemned to inhabit an ' accursed valley ' in which they shall undergo punishment. Here we find the repulsive idea that the torments of the wicked in Gehenna will be a spectacle for the satisfaction of the righteous : ' And in the last days there will be the spectacle of a righteous judgement upon them, in the presence of the righteous continually for ever : here will those who have found mercy bless the Lord of glory, the eternal King. And in the days of judgement over the former, they will bless Him for the mercy in accordance with which He has assigned them their lot ' (xxvii). This idea is probably based upon the writer's interpretation of the last verse of the Book of Isaiah, a passage which we noticed when dealing with the Book of Daniel.

The most noteworthy point with regard to this conception of the Messianic age which is to ensue after the great judgement is that it is pictured as an earthly kingdom, and the lives of those who share in it, though they will be prolonged to a patriarchal age, will apparently at last be terminated by death in the natural course of events.

So in xxv. 6 we read : ' [The elect] will rejoice with joy and be glad : they will enter the holy habitation : the fragrance thereof will be in their limbs, and they will live a long life on earth, such as thy fathers have lived : and in their days no sorrow or pain or calamity will affect them.'

The writer, then, is merely looking forward to a Messianic future such as is pictured in Isaiah lxv, lxvi, when the present anomalies of justice will be rectified.   What is finally in store for the souls of the righteous after they have enjoyed the bliss of the Messianic Kingdom up to a good old age he does not tell us ; but apparently he has no conception of the doctrine of the immortality of the soul—at any rate there is no hint of it in his Apocalypse.

We must now pass on to the second section of Enoch in chronological order : chapters lxxxiii–xc, dated by Dr. Charles B.C. 166–161.   Here Enoch is represented as communicating to his son Methuselah the revelation which he has received, not, as in the first section, through direct intercourse with the holy angels, but through the medium of visions.

The history of the chosen race is traced from the beginning in symbolical language, sin, as in the first section, being referred to the fallen angels. The writer narrates, under the garb of symbol, the rise and struggle of the Maccabaean patriots ; hence he must have written when the Chasîdim were still in sympathy with the Maccabees ; and this is the reason why the section is dated in the period between B.C. 166–161, shortly after the composition of the Book of Daniel. The main interest of the writer centres round Israel's history after the Exile. It is true that Israel has sinned grievously ; but their punishment has been disproportionately heavier than their guilt. This is due to the seventy shepherds into whose hand God committed His sheep, but who failed to observe the Divine commands and ' began to slay and destroy more than they were bidden, and delivered those sheep into the hands of the lions ' (lxxxix. 59 ff.). There is some obscurity as to the shepherds, but there can be little doubt that they represent superhuman and not human guardians, i.e. angelic powers. Deliverance is to come through the efforts of the Maccabaean patriots, supplemented by Divine assistance at the most critical juncture, when the earth opens and swallows up Israel's foes : ' And I saw till the Lord of the sheep came unto them and took the staff of His wrath into His hand and smote the earth so that it was rent asunder, and all the beasts and the birds of the heaven fell away from the sheep, and sank in the earth and it closed over them' (xc. 18). Soon follows the judgement: ' And I saw till a throne was erected in the pleasant land, and the Lord of the sheep sat Himself thereon, and that other took the sealed books and opened them before the Lord of the sheep ' (xc. 20). The Lord then calls ' those seven white

ones ', i. e. apparently an order of seven arch-
angels, a conception derived from the Zoroastrian
Amshaspands, and they bring before Him the
fallen angels and the guilty shepherds, who are
bound and cast into the fiery abyss, together with
the blinded sheep, i. e. the Jewish apostates, who
have sinned and been found guilty.   Then the
old house, i. e. the old Jerusalem, is folded up and
replaced by ' a new house greater and loftier than
the first ', which is ' set up in the place of the first
that had been folded up '.   Into this new Jerusalem, within which is ' the Lord of the sheep ', the
elect sheep are gathered.   ' And all that had been
destroyed and dispersed, and all the beasts of the
field, and all the birds of the heaven assembled in
that house, and the Lord of the sheep rejoiced
with great joy because they were all good and had
returned to His house ' (xc. 33).   Here we have
the new Jerusalem peopled with the surviving
elect of Israel and with the righteous dead, together
with the Gentiles who have been converted (xc. 30),
typified by the beasts of the field and the birds of
the heaven.   After this the Messiah (typified by a
white bull) is born and assumes dominion of the
kingdom, and all the inhabitants of the kingdom
are restored to the primitive righteousness of man's
first parents.

Here we notice, as an advance on the conceptions
of Section I, the change of the old earthly
Jerusalem into the heavenly new Jerusalem as the
only fitting abode of God.   Further, the resurrec-

tion is limited to the righteous dead only. Thus,
as Dr. Charles remarks, ' our writer holds fast to
the original and spiritual view of the resurrection,
that the risen life is the organic development of
the righteous life on earth.' Lastly, the righteous
are transformed into the image of the Messiah.
This appears in the writer's quaint symbolism :
' I saw till all their (different) kinds were transformed and they all became white oxen ; and
the first among them became the buffalo, and that
buffalo became a great animal, and had great black
horns on its head ; and the Lord of the sheep
rejoiced over them and over all the oxen.' From
this transformation of the righteous, and from the
fact that no limit is placed to the duration of their
lives, we are probably justified in assuming that
the writer is picturing the new form of existence
as eternal life in the fullest sense.

In the third section, chapters xci–civ, Enoch
addresses his descendants, and unfolds to them
the course of history under the symbol of so many
weeks. The first seven weeks are occupied with
the events of the world up to the establishment
of the Messianic Kingdom. This kingdom is
temporary merely, and is followed (and not
preceded) by the great judgement. It terminates
in the tenth week, and is superseded by a period
when ' the first heaven will depart and pass away,
and a new heaven will appear, and all the powers
of the heavens will shine sevenfold for ever. And
after that there will be many weeks without

number for ever in goodness and righteousness, and sin will no more be mentioned for ever (xci. 16, 17).

Here we find a more transcendental view of the future in store for the righteous. The earthly Messianic Kingdom is no longer regarded as fit to satisfy the spiritual aspirations of the righteous. These can only find their goal in the heavenly life which is to last ' many weeks without number ', i. e. for ever.

The remainder of the section takes the form of an argument in which it is shown that earthly prosperity has nothing whatever to do with righteousness. The arguments of the writer's Sadducean opponents are brought up in the form of statements in the mouths of ' sinners ' only to be refuted and overthrown, and it is proved that only in the future blessedness of eternal life can the suffering righteous meet with their true reward. The date of this section is drawn from the inference that the breach between the Maccabees represented by John Hyrcanus, and the Chasîdim or Pharisaic party, must have taken place. Events had shown that not much was to be hoped from the establishment of an earthly kingdom, and that it was upon the heavenly life that the righteous must set their hopes for a glorious future.

The fourth section, chapters xxxvii–lxx, is the most important and interesting in the whole book, as regards the development of the doctrine of a future life. The date is decided by the references to the kings and mighty ones who shed the blood of the righteous and who were supported by the Sadducean party. These can only be the later Maccabaean princes ; for since the blood of the Chasîdim was not shed by the Maccabaeans before B.C. 95, and the Herodians, on the other hand, had not the support of the Sadducees, we obtain B. C. 95 as the earliest date, and B. C. 64 (the date of the interposition of Rome in the affairs of Judea) as the latest possible date.

This section takes the form of three ' Similitudes ' imparted to Enoch, the term ' similitude ' standing, as is often the case with the Greek παραβολή and the Hebrew מָשָׁל, for an ' elaborate discourse, whether in the form of a vision, a prophecy, or a poem '. These Similitudes narrate the course of events which will come to pass at the final judgement. The author holds fast to the idea of a Messianic Kingdom; but he spiritualizes the conception and transfers its scene from the present earthly stage to a new heaven and a new earth. Most important of all, the conception of the Messiah is spiritualized. He is no longer merely human, but He appears as a supernatural Person, endowed with Divine attributes. Four titles are applied to Him—' the Christ,' ' the Righteous One,' ' the Elect One,' and, most frequently and noticeably of all, ' the Son of Man.' This latter title as here employed appears to be the true origin of the title as used by our Lord of Himself.

In summarizing the attributes of the Messiah, I cannot do better than quote the words of Dr. Charles in his *Eschatology*, p. 215 f. :—

' The Messiah is conceived in the Similitudes as (i) the Judge of the world and the Revealer of all things ; (ii) the Messianic Champion and Ruler of the righteous. (i) As Judge, He possesses righteousness, wisdom and power. He is the Righteous One in an extraordinary sense (xxxviii. 2 ; liii. 6) ; He possesses righteousness, and it dwells with Him (xlvi. 3), and on the ground of His essential righteousness (xlvi. 3) has He been chosen no less than according to God's good pleasure (xlix. 4). Wisdom, which could find no dwelling-place on earth (xlii), dwells in Him, and the spirit of Him who giveth knowledge (xlix. 3) ; and the secrets of wisdom stream forth from His mouth (li. 3), and wisdom is poured forth like water before Him (xlix). In Him abides the spirit of power (xlix. 3), and He possesses universal dominion (lxii. 6). He is the revealer of all things. His appearance will be the signal for the revelation of good and the unmasking of evil ; will bring to light everything that is hidden, alike the invisible world of righteousness and the hidden world of sin (xlvi. 3 ; xlix. 2, 4) ; and will recall to life those who have perished on land and sea, and those that are in She'ol and hell (li. 1 ; lxi. 5). Evil when once unmasked will vanish from His presence (xlix. 2). Hence all judgement has been committed unto Him (lxix. 27) and universal dominion (lxii. 6), and He will sit on the throne of His glory (xlv. 3 ; lxii. 3, 5), which is likewise the throne of God (xlvii. 3 ; li. 3), and all men, righteous and wicked, and all angels, fallen and unfallen, will be judged before Him (li. 2 ; lv. 4 ; lxi. 8 ; lxii. 2, 3), and no lying utterance will be possible before Him (xlix. 4 ; lxii. 3), and by the mere word of His mouth will He slay the ungodly (lxii. 2).

' (ii) He is the Messianic Champion and Ruler of the righteous. He is the stay of the righteous (xlviii. 4), and has already been revealed to them (lxii. 7); He is the avenger of their life (xlvii. 7), the preserver of their inheritance (xlviii. 7) ; He will vindicate the earth as their possession for ever (li. 5), and establish the community of the righteous in unhindered prosperity (liii. 6 ; lxii. 8) ; their faces will shine with joy (li. 5), and they will be vestured with life (lxii. 15), and be resplendent with light (xxxix. 7), and " become angels in heaven " (li. 4), and He will abide in closest communion with them for ever (lxii. 14), in the immediate presence of the Lord of Spirits (xxxix. 7), and His glory is for ever and ever, and His might unto all generations (xlix. 2).'

In summarizing the attributes of the Messiah, we summarize at the same time the writer's doctrine of a future life in store for the righteous ; and where the whole section is so important in its bearing on this doctrine, space will not permit me to select any particular portion by way of further illustration of the writer's conception. It may, however, be gathered, even from a mere summary, how important the Similitudes are in their spiritualized conception of the Messianic hope, and in transference of its scene from earth to the Kingdom of Heaven. It will be clear, also, that this section must have been familiar to our Lord, and must largely have influenced the form into which He cast His teaching with regard to His position and office as 'Son of Man', and with regard to the Kingdom of Heaven which He came to establish. It is indeed remarkable and significant that such an Apocalypse should have been put forward at a period so shortly removed from the destined realization of the writer's aspirations 'in the fullness of time'.

At this point we must conclude our brief survey of Apocalyptic. We have seen that the hope of immortality, previously existent only as the aspiration or conviction of individuals, assumes in this literature the definite form of a resurrection for the elect ; taking shape along lines which are often crude and unsightly, but gradually become shaped and spiritualized so as to form no unworthy medium for the teaching of Him who came to abolish death and to bring life and incorruptibility to light through the Gospel.

At the same time, it is no subject for regret that later Apocalyptic, even when it took the spiritualized form of the Similitudes, finds no place in the Old Testament Canon. Such attempts to penetrate into things unseen could never possess the

lasting spiritual worth and satisfaction which is
inherent in the personal conviction of the individual
soul as to the meaning of its communion with God.
It is the realization of *this* that gives permanency to
the Psalmist's expression of his faith :—

Nevertheless, I am continually with Thee,
Thou hast holden my right hand.
According to Thy purpose wilt Thou lead me,
And afterwards wilt take me gloriously.
Whom have I in heaven ?
And, having Thee, there is naught that I desire upon
      earth ;
Though my flesh and my heart should have wasted away,
God would be the Rock of my heart, and my portion
      for ever !

This conviction of a personal relation to God
independent of time and change, and not any
particular theory as to the character of the life
after death, is the lasting contribution of the Old
Testament to the doctrine of a Future Life. It is
this aspect of the Hope which is taken up, enlarged,
and emphasized in the New Testament. Our Lord
Himself, who seems to have discouraged curious
inquiry as to the number of the saved and the
details of the future judgement, has much to say
about that present condition of personal communion
with God which it was His human mission to realize,
and names it Eternal Life as carrying with it the
assurance of unbroken continuity into the unseen
future :—'This is life eternal, that they should
know Thee the only true God, and Him whom
Thou didst send, even Jesus Christ' (S. John

xvii. 3); 'He that heareth My word, and believeth Him that sent Me, hath eternal life, and cometh not into judgement, but hath passed out of death into life' (S. John v. 24).

Thus, however germinal in character Israel's Hope of Immortality may seem to have been, it yet contains within itself the promise and potency of the Gospel, and links itself on to that assured conviction of our Faith which has its basis in a present union with God through Jesus Christ, and which must ever meet and satisfy the highest aspirations of the human soul.

www.ingramcontent.com/pod-product-compliance
Lightning Source LLC
LaVergne TN
LVHW021611080426
835510LV00019B/2510